Heroines of the Past
Bible Study

Heroines of the Past Bible Study

An Inspiring Thirteen-Week Virtue Study
Celebrating the Noble Deeds of
Women and Girls from History

By Amy Puetz

Golden Prairie Press
History at its Best!

Golden Prairie Press
P.O. Box 429
Wright, WY 82732

www.AmyPuetz.com

Cover & Layout Design by Amy Puetz
Cover image: "A Good Book" by Henry Lejeune

ISBN: 978-0-9825199-7-4

Copyright 2012 by Amy Puetz
All Rights Reserved
No part of this book may be reproduced in any form or by any electronic or mechanical means including information storage and retrieval systems, without permission in writing from the author. The only exception is by a reviewer, who may quote short excerpts in a review.

CONTENTS

Introduction..ix

~ WEEK 1 ~
Day 1: The Courage of Princess Edith, Part 1..............................1
Day 2: The Courage of Princess Edith, Part 2..............................5
Day 3: The Courage of Princess Edith, Part 3..............................9
Day 4: The Courage of Princess Edith, Part 4............................13
Day 5: A Brave Little Girl..17

~ WEEK 2 ~
Day 1: Living and Dying for Jesus, Part 1..................................21
Day 2: Living and Dying for Jesus, Part 2..................................25
Day 3: The Heroine of Fort Henry, Part 1...................................29
Day 4: The Heroine of Fort Henry, Part 2...................................33
Day 5: Thwarting the British...37

~ WEEK 3 ~
Day 1: Mary Slessor, a Dundee Factory Girl..............................41
Day 2: Mary Slessor the Missionary, Part 1................................45
Day 3: Mary Slessor the Missionary, Part 2................................49
Day 4: Mary Slessor of Calabar...53
Day 5: Two Girls Who Braved the Sea.......................................57

~ WEEK 4 ~
Day 1: The American Army of Two..61
Day 2: The Mother of Andrew Jackson, Part 1...........................65
Day 3: The Mother of Andrew Jackson, Part 2...........................69
Day 4: Marcelle and the Great War...73
Day 5: Felicitas, a First-Century Christian of Rome...................77

~ WEEK 5 ~
Day 1: An Indian Princess Guide, Part 1..................................81
Day 2: An Indian Princess Guide, Part 2..................................85
Day 3: An Indian Princess Guide, Part 3..................................89
Day 4: An Indian Princess Guide, Part 4..................................93
Day 5: A Providential Escape...97

~ WEEK 6 ~
Day 1: A Kind Woman Who Helped Luther.............................101
Day 2: Running to the Truth...105
Day 3: The Wife of Martin Luther, Part 1................................109
Day 4: The Wife of Martin Luther, Part 2................................113
Day 5: Luther's Little Girl..117

~ WEEK 7 ~
Day 1: Keeper of the Light...121
Day 2: Princess Sarah, Part 1..125
Day 3: Princess Sarah, Part 2..129
Day 4: Princess Sarah, Part 3..133
Day 5: The Compassionate Nurse, Part 1..............................137

~ WEEK 8 ~
Day 1: The Compassionate Nurse, Part 2..............................141
Day 2: Captured by Indians, Part 1.......................................145
Day 3: Captured by Indians, Part 2.......................................149
Day 4: The Warrior Mother, Part 1..155
Day 5: The Warrior Mother, Part 2..159

~ WEEK 9 ~
Day 1: The Valiant Maid of Orleans, Part 1............................163
Day 2: The Valiant Maid of Orleans, Part 2............................167
Day 3: The Valiant Maid of Orleans, Part 3............................171
Day 4: The Valiant Maid of Orleans, Part 4............................175
Day 5: The Valiant Maid of Orleans, Part 5............................179

~ WEEK 10 ~

Day 1: The Little Nurse, Part 1..183
Day 2: The Little Nurse, Part 2..187
Day 3: Florence Nightingale and the Party.................................191
Day 4: The Lady with the Lamp...195
Day 5: The Heroine of the Alamo...199

~ WEEK 11 ~

Day 1: The Lady Who Loved to Learn......................................203
Day 2: The Nine Days' Queen, Part 1...207
Day 3: The Nine Days' Queen, Part 2...211
Day 4: Battling for the Boys in Blue, Part 1...............................215
Day 5: Battling for the Boys in Blue, Part 2...............................219

~ WEEK 12 ~

Day 1: Upheaval in China, Part 1..223
Day 2: Upheaval in China, Part 2..227
Day 3: Upheaval in China, Part 3..231
Day 4: Upheaval in China, Part 4..235
Day 5: An Indian Princess of the Forest......................................239

~ WEEK 13 ~

Day 1: The Saving of Clotilda..243
Day 2: The Service of Clotilda..247
Day 3: The Husband of Clotilda...251
Day 4: The Hiding Place...255
Day 5: Grace Darling's Heroic Deed...259

List of Virtues..263

LIST OF HEROINES IN THIS BOOK

Abbie Burgess, who kept the light at Matinicus Rock burning	121
Blandina, a Christian slave girl in Lyons	21
Clotilda, a princess and queen in the fifth century	243
Edith Cavell, a nurse during World War I	137
Edith, princess of Scotland, also known as Good Queen Maud	1
Elizabeth Hutchinson Jackson, the mother of Andrew Jackson	65
Elizabeth Zane, the heroine of Fort Henry	29
Felicitas, a first-century Christian in Rome	77
Florence Nightingale, a famous nurse	137
Grace Darling, who saved a group of shipwrecked men	259
Grace Vernon Bussell, who saved those who were shipwrecked	57
Helen Patterson, who was captured by Indians and escaped	97
Helen Petrie, who saved two drowning men	58
Jane de Montfort, the mother who preserved her son's inheritance	155
Jennie Crawford and Jennie Cody, missionaries in China	223
Joan of Arc, who fought for France	163
Katherine von Bora Luther, the wife of Martin Luther	105
Lady Jane Grey, the girl who was queen for nine days	203
Magdalena Luther, the daughter of Martin Luther	117
Marcelle Semmer, a French heroine of World War I	73
Mary Slessor, who was a missionary in Africa	41
Mother Bickerdyke, a woman who nursed boys in the Civil War	215
Peggy Miller, who carried a message for the Continental Army	263
Pocahontas, a Powhatan Indian princess	239
Polly Daggett, who thwarted the English	37
Polly Hopkins, who ran for help when Indians attacked her family	255
Rebecca and Abigail Bates, who frightened the English	61
Regina Leininger, who was captured by Indians	145
Sacagawea, who guided Lewis and Clark across the continent	81
Sarah Winnemucca, a Paiute princess who helped keep the peace	125
Susanna Dickenson, who survived the Alamo	199
Ursula Cotta, a German woman who encouraged Martin Luther	101

INTRODUCTION

I'm so excited to share the stories in this book with you! One day I was talking with a lovely Christian woman who asked me if I'd ever written a Bible study for girls. I told her that I'd thought about it before but had never actually started. She encouraged me to write one because she saw a need for such books, and the book you are holding now is the result of that conversation. That is what Christian women and girls are supposed to do for each other: encourage their sisters in Christ to follow God and grow spiritually.

As I put this book together, I met lots of amazing, virtuous ladies who inspired me. There are hundreds of old stories that have been unpublished for years, and I'm excited to be republishing some of them for a whole new generation to discover. Each day of this study has a short story about a historical lady. Following that is a Bible study, where you will read Scriptures that talk about that lady's virtues. I encourage you to make this experience as special as possible. I created this study to be used by a mother and daughter but it could also be used for a personal Bible study or in a

Sunday school class. For a large class you could have the girls do the daily readings at home and then talk about what they learned during the class. If you are doing the study as a mother and daughter, consider buying pretty notebooks or journals to write down your answers to the study questions. If you're studying on your own, brew a cup of tea and enjoy it while you do your daily reading. This book is a tool that can open up doors to deeper discussions: if a subject comes up while doing the study, take time to learn more about it.

If you are studying as a group, keep in mind that many of the stories in this book would be fun to dramatize. Use the dialogue where provided, and ad lib the rest.

Another element of this study is the "box of visual reminders" which is referenced in some lessons. This box could be made during the first day. All you need is a box (a shoebox would work well) covered with fabric or pretty pictures. In this box, you will put things that remind you of important truths. I have several suggestions throughout the book of what to put in the box, but feel free to be creative and add your own items.

Have fun, and enjoy learning about these truly noble hearts. May they point you toward your Creator, Jesus Christ. For no matter how virtuous a woman is, her characteristics pale in comparison to our perfect Lord.

I hope and pray this book will bless you on your journey through life.

Pilgrim on a journey,
Amy Puetz

WEEK 1 ~ DAY 1

The Courage of Princess Edith, Part 1
By E.S. Brooks, 1887

During the turbulent years of the Middle Ages, a beautiful young princess lived. She would later be remembered as a great queen, but in her youth she was known simply as Princess Edith.

On a broad and deep window seat in the old Abbey guesthouse at Gloucester sat two young girls, aged thirteen and ten. Before them, brave-looking enough in his old-time costume, stood a manly young fellow of sixteen. The three were in earnest conversation, unmindful of the noise about them created by the chatter of young people, attendants, and followers of the knights and barons of King William's court.

William Rufus, son of William the Conqueror and second Norman king of England, held his summer council in the curious old Roman-Saxon-Norman town of Gloucester, in the fair valley through which flows the noble Severn. It was held in the old Benedictine Abbey, while the court was lodged in the Abbey guesthouses, in the stately Gloucester Castle, and in the houses of the quaint old town itself.

The boy was shaking his head rather doubtfully as he stood looking down upon the two girls on the broad window seat.

"Nay, nay, sir, shake not your head like that," exclaimed the younger of the girls. "We did escape that way, trust me we did, Edith here can tell you I do speak the truth—for sure, 'twas her device."

Thirteen-year-old Edith laughed cheerfully enough at her sister's confusion, and said merrily as the lad turned questioningly to her, "Sure, then, sir, 'tis plain to see that you are Southern-born and know not the nature of a Scottish mist. Yet 'tis even as Mary said. For, as we have told you, the Maiden's Castle stands high on the crag in Edwin's Burgh and hath many concealed pathways to the lower gate. So when the Red Donald's men were swarming up the steep, my uncle, Atheling, did guide us by ways we knew well, and by twists and turnings that none knew better, straight through Red Donald's troops, and unseen by them because of the blessed thickness of the gathering mist."

"And this was your device?" asked the boy admiringly.

"Aye, but anyone might have devised it too," replied young Edith modestly. "Sure, 'twas no great device to use a Scottish mist for our safety, and 'twere wiser to chance it than stay and be murdered by Red Donald's men. And so it was, good Robert, even as Mary did say, that we came forth unharmed from amidst them and fled here to King William's court, where we are safe at last."

"Safe, say you—safe?" exclaimed the lad impulsively. "Aye, as safe as is a mouse's nest in a cat's corner. But that I know you to be a brave and resolute maid, I should say to you—"

But before Edith could know what he would say, their conference was rudely broken in upon. For a royal page, dashing up to the three, with scant courtesy seized the arm of the elder girl and said hurriedly, "Haste ye, haste ye, my lady! Our lord king is even now calling for you to come before him in the banquet hall."

Edith knew too well the rough manners of those dangerous days. She freed herself from the grasp of the page and said, "Nay, that may I not, master page. 'Tis neither safe nor seemly for a maid to show herself in a baron's hall or in a king's banquet room."

"Safe and seemly it may not be, but come you must," said the page rudely. "The king demands it, and your reluctance is worthless."

And so, hurried along whether she would or no, while her friend, Robert Fitz Godwine, accompanied her as far as he dared, the young Princess Edith was speedily brought into the presence of the king of England, William II, called, from the color of his hair and from his fiery temper, Rufus, or "the Red."

For Edith and Mary were both princesses of Scotland, with a history, even before they had reached their teens, as romantic as it was exciting. Their mother, an exiled Saxon princess, had, after the conquest of Saxon England by the firm Duke William the Norman, found refuge in Scotland. She had there married King Malcolm Canmore, the son of that King Duncan whom Macbeth had slain. But when King Malcolm had fallen beneath the walls of Alnwick Castle, a victim to English treachery, and when his fierce brother Donald Bane, or Donald the Red, had usurped the throne of Scotland, then the good Queen Margaret died in the gray castle on the rock of Edinburgh. The five orphaned children were only saved from the vengeance of their bad uncle Donald by the shrewd and daring device of the young Princess Edith, who bade their good uncle Edgar, the Atheling, guide them under cover of the mist straight through the Red Donald's knights and spearmen to England and safety.

Virtue Study

Memory Verse: Proverbs 31:10. Write this verse on a 3 x 5 card and memorize it during the week.

Share your thoughts about the questions below.

1. Why was Edith in Gloucester?
2. How did she and her family escape?
3. What are some of the virtues mentioned in this chapter?

What do these verses say about courage? Where does true courage come from?
- Philippians 1:20
- Hebrews 3:6

Edith's family was saved by her quick thinking. Does her story of escape remind you of anyone in the Bible? (Read 1 Samuel 19:11–18 and 2 Samuel 17:17–22 for a couple of examples.) Read those passages and answer these questions.
- Who escaped?
- How did they get away?
- Why were they in trouble?

The days of brave knights and fair maidens may be long gone, but the virtues they possessed are still alive and well. What are some noble ways you could help your family do everyday activities? Could you offer to help your mom do the dishes? Could you take care of a younger sibling? Could you tell an older sibling that you like something he or she did? Think of a couple of things to do today to help or encourage your family.

WEEK 1 ~ DAY 2

The Courage of Princess Edith, Part 2
By E.S. Brooks, 1887

Perhaps the worst possible place for the fugitives to seek safety was in Norman England, for Edgar the Atheling, a Saxon prince, had twice been declared king of England by the Saxon enemies of the Norman conquerors, and the children of King Malcolm and Queen Margaret—half-Scottish, half-Saxon—were, by blood and birth, a threat to the conquerors. But the Red King in his rough sort of way—hot today and cold tomorrow—had shown something almost like friendship for this Saxon Atheling, or royal prince, who might have been king of England had he not wisely submitted to the greater power of William the Conqueror and to the Red William, his son. More than this, it had been rumored that some two years before, when there was a truce between the kings of England and of Scotland, this harsh and headstrong English king, who was as rough and repelling as a chestnut burr, had seen, noticed, and expressed a particular interest in the eleven-year-old Scottish girl—this very Princess Edith who now sought his protection.

So when this wandering uncle boldly threw himself upon Norman courtesy and came with his homeless nephews and nieces straight to the Norman court for safety, King William Rufus not only received these children with favor and a royal welcome, but gave them comfortable rooms in the quaint old town of Gloucester, where he held his court.

Just when the royal fugitives deemed themselves safest were they in the greatest danger.

Among the attendant knights and nobles of King William's court was a Saxon knight known as Sir Ordgar, a thane (or baronet) of Oxfordshire, and because those who change their opinions—political or otherwise—often prove the most unrelenting enemies of their former associates, it came to pass that Sir Ordgar, the Saxon, conceived a strong dislike for these orphaned descendants of the Saxon kings. He convinced himself that the best way to secure himself in the good graces of the Norman King William was to slander and accuse the children of the Saxon Queen Margaret.

So that very day in the great hall, when wine was flowing and passions were strong, this false knight, raising his glass, bade them all drink, "Confusion to the enemies of our liege the king, from the base Philip of France to the baser Edgar the Atheling and his Scottish brats!"

This was an insult that even the peace-loving nature of Edgar the Atheling could not brook. He sprang to his feet and denounced the charge. "None here is truer or more loyal to you, Lord King," he said, "than am I, Edgar the Atheling, and my charges, your guests."

However, King William Rufus was of that changing temper that goes with jealousy and suspicion. His flushed face grew still redder, and, turning away from the Saxon prince, he demanded, "Why make you this charge, Sir Ordgar?"

"Because of its truth, sire," said the faithless knight. "For what other cause hath this false Atheling sought sanctuary here, save to use his own descent from the ancient kings of this realm to plot against your majesty? And his eldest kinsgirl here, the Princess Edith, hath she not been spreading a story among the younger folk, of how some old woman hath said that she who is the daughter of kings shall be the wife and mother of kings? And is it not further true that when her aunt, the Abbess of Romsey, bade her wear the holy veil, she hath again and yet again torn it off, and said that she, who was to be a queen, could never be made a nun? Children and fools, 'tis said, do speak the truth, sire. And in all this do I see the malice of this false Atheling, the friend of your rebellious brother Duke Robert, as you do know him to be, and I do brand him here, in this presence, as traitor and disloyal to you, his lord."

The anger of the jealous king grew more unreasoning as Sir Ordgar went on.

"Enough!" he cried. "Seize the traitor, or stay. Children and fools, as you have said, Sir Ordgar, do indeed speak the truth. Have in the girl and let us hear the truth. Not seemly? Sir Atheling—" he broke out in reply to some protest of Edith's uncle. "Aught is seemly that the king doth wish. Raoul! Damian! My pages! Run, one of you, and seek the Princess Edith, and bring her here forthwith!"

While Edgar the Atheling tried, though without effect, to reason with the angry king, Damian the page hurried after the Princess Edith.

Virtue Study

Work on Proverbs 31:10, the memory verse for this week.

1. What were the character flaws of King William Rufus?
2. Why did Princess Edith go to his court?
3. Did she know the danger she would face?

What warnings and promises are found in these verses?
- ♥ Proverbs 9:7–9
- ♥ Proverbs 12:3
- ♥ Proverbs 12:20
- ♥ Proverbs 14:14–18
- ♥ Proverbs 15:1–2

Does Edith's situation remind you of a Bible character? (Read 1 Samuel 19:1–10 for an example.)

WEEK 1 ~ DAY 3

The Courage of Princess Edith, Part 3
By E.S. Brooks, 1887

"How now, mistress!" broke out the Red King as the young girl was ushered into the banquet hall, where the disordered tables, strewn with fragments of the feast, showed the rough manners of those brutal days. "How now, mistress! Do you talk of kings and queens and of your own designs—you, who are but a beggar guest? Is it seemly or wise to talk—nay, keep you quiet, Sir Atheling, we will have naught from you—to talk of thrones and crowns as if you did even now hope to win the realm from me—from me, your only protector?"

The Princess Edith was a very high-spirited maiden, and this unexpected accusation, instead of frightening her, only served to embolden her. She looked the angry monarch full in the face.

"'Tis a false and lying charge, Lord King," she said, "from whomsoever it may come. Naught have I said but praise of you and your courtesy to us motherless folk. 'Tis a false and lying charge. I am ready to stand test of its proving, come what may."

"Even to the judgment of God, girl?" demanded the king.

The brave girl made instant reply. "Even to the judgment of God, Lord King." Then, skilled in all the curious customs of those warlike times, she drew off her glove. "Whosoever my accuser be, Lord King," she said, "I do denounce him as deceptive and false, and thus do I throw myself upon God's good mercy, if it shall please him to raise me up a champion." And she flung her glove upon the floor of the hall, in the face of the king and all his barons.

It was a bold thing for a girl to do, and a murmur of applause ran through even that unfriendly throng. For to stand the test of a wager of battle, or the "judgment of God," as the savage contest was called, was the last resort of anyone accused of treason or of crime. It meant no less than a duel to the death between the accuser and the accused or their accepted champions, and upon the result of the duel hung the lives of those in dispute. The Princess Edith's glove, lying on the floor of the Abbey hall, was her declaration that she had spoken the truth and was willing to risk her life in proof of her innocence.

Edgar the Atheling, peace-lover though he was, would gladly have accepted the post of champion for his niece, but as one also involved in the charge of treason, such action was denied him.

For the moment, the Red King's former admiration for this brave young princess caused him to waver—but those were days when suspicion and jealousy rose above all nobler traits. His face grew stern again.

"Ordgar of Oxford," he said, "take up the glove!" And Edith knew who her enemy was. Then the king asked, "Who stands as champion for Edgar the Atheling and this maid, his niece?"

Almost before the words were spoken, young Robert Fitz Godwine had sprung to Edith's side.

"That would I, Lord King, if a young squire might appear against a belted knight!"

"Ordgar of Oxford fights not with boys!" said the accuser scornfully.

The king's savage humor broke out again.

"Face him with your own page, Sir Ordgar," he said with a grim laugh. "Boy against boy would be a fitting wager for a young maid's life."

However, the Saxon knight was in no mood for sport. "Nay, sire, this is no child's play," he said. "I care nothing for this girl. I stand as champion for the king against yon traitor Atheling, and if the maiden's cause is his, why then against her too. This is a man's quarrel."

Young Robert would have spoken yet again, as his face flushed hot with anger at the knight's sneering words. But a firm hand was laid upon his shoulder, and a strong voice said, "Then is it mine, Sir Ordgar. If between man and man, then will I, with the gracious permission of our lord the king, stand as champion for this maiden here and for my good lord, the noble Atheling, whose liegeman and whose man am I, next to you, Lord King." And taking the mate to the glove which the Princess Edith had flung down in defiance, he thrust it into the guard of his iron cap, in token that he, Godwine of Winchester, the father of the boy Robert, was the young girl's champion.

Virtue Study

Work on Proverbs 31:10, the memory verse for this week.

1. What virtues did Princess Edith display?
2. If Princess Edith had been guilty of plotting against the king, could she have been so bold in her response? Why or why not?

Princess Edith was not prepared to defend herself before King William. In the book of Matthew, Jesus tells His followers what to do if they are brought into court for being His disciples. Read Matthew 10:17–20. What should a Christian do in this situation? Read Acts 6:8–7:60, where a Christian's trial takes place.

Box of Visual Reminders

Make or buy a box to place items in during this Bible study. (A shoebox is about the right size.) An idea would be to take a shoebox and cover it with pretty pictures. As we go through this study, we will collect items that remind us of truths found in God's Word.

During the Middle Ages, when a girl or woman was charged with a crime, she could request a champion to fight against her accuser. If her champion was the winner, she was set free; but if her accuser was successful, she would be punished. Often, the penalty would be death. In a similar way, God sent His Son, Jesus Christ, to be our Champion. We were guilty of sinning against God, but instead of seeing us punished, Jesus paid the price for our freedom.

Place a glove (any kind of glove will work) in the box. Every time you see it, remember that Christ is our Champion.

WEEK 1 ~ DAY 4

The Courage of Princess Edith, Part 4
By E.S. Brooks, 1887

Three days after, in the yard of Gloucester Castle, the wager of battle was fought. It was no happy tournament such as are described in the stories of romance and chivalry, with streaming banners, brightly dressed ladies, flower-bedecked balconies, and all the splendid display of a tournament of the knights. It was a solemn and somber gathering in which all the arrangements suggested only death and gloom, while the accused waited in suspense, knowing that death by fire was prepared for them should their champion fall. The glove of each contestant was flung into the combat field by the judge, and the dispute was committed for settlement to the power of God and their own good swords. Such combat is a stirring picture of those days of daring and of might, when force took the place of justice and the deadliest blows were the only persuasive arguments. Though supported by the favor of the king and a display of splendid armor, Ordgar's treachery had its just reward. Virtue triumphed, and vice was punished. Even while treacherously endeavoring to stab the brave Godwine with a knife which he had concealed in his boot, the false Sir Ordgar was overcome, confessed the falsehood of his charge against Edgar the Atheling and Edith his niece, and, as the quaint old record has it, "The strength of his grief and the multitude of his wounds drove out his impious soul."

So young Edith was saved, and, as is usually the case with men of his character, the Red King's humor changed completely. The victorious Godwine received the arms and lands of the dead Ordgar. Edgar the Atheling was raised high in trust and honor. The throne of Scotland, wrested from the Red Donald, was placed once more in the family of King Malcolm, and King William Rufus himself became the guardian and protector of the Princess Edith.

One fatal August day, the Red King was found pierced by an arrow under the trees of the New Forest. His younger brother, Duke Henry, whom men called Beauclerc, "the good scholar," for his love of learning and of books, ascended the throne of England as King Henry I. And the very year of his accession, on the 11th of November, 1100, in the Abbey of Westminster he married the Princess Edith of Scotland, then a fair young lady of scarce twenty-one. At the request of her husband, she took the Norman name of Matilda, or Maud, upon her coronation day, and by this name she is known in history and among the queens of England.

Barely thirty-four years after the Norman Conquest, a Saxon princess sat upon the throne of Norman England, the loving wife of the son of the very man by whom Saxon England was conquered.

"Never, since the Battle of Hastings," says Sir Francis Palgrave, the historian, "had there been such a joyous day as when Queen Maud was crowned." Victors and vanquished, Normans and Saxons, were united at last, and the name of "Good Queen Maud" was long an honored memory among the people of England.

And she was a good queen. In a time of bitter tyranny, when the common people were but the serfs and slaves of the haughty and cruel barons, this young queen labored to bring in kindlier manners and more gentle ways. Beautiful in face, she was still more lovely in heart and life. Her influence upon her husband, Henry the Scholar, was seen in the wise laws he made, and the Charter of King Henry is said to have been gained by her suggestion. This important paper was the first step toward popular liberty. It led the way to the Magna Charta, and finally to our own Declaration of Independence. The girls of America, therefore, can look back with interest and affection upon the romantic story of Good Queen Maud, the brave-hearted girl who showed herself wise and fearless both in the perilous mist at Edinburgh and later still, in the yet-greater dangers of her trial at Gloucester.

Virtue Study

Work on Proverbs 31:10, the memory verse for this week.

1. How was Edith saved?
2. What happened to her when she grew up?
3. What are some of the virtues Princess Edith displayed?

Princess Edith trusted in God to protect her. King David also knew that trusting in God was the only way to be free from fear. Read Psalm 27 and answer these questions:
- ♥ How does David describe God in verse 1?
- ♥ What promises are found in verse 5?
- ♥ In verse 11, what does David ask God to do?
- ♥ How did David find confidence in verse 13?
- ♥ What are we told to do in verse 14?

Have you ever been in a situation where you needed to be brave? What did you do? Write about the experience and how God helped you through.

Princess Edith grew up to be Good Queen Maud. She must have been kind, compassionate, and wise to be remembered as "good." Many people in history are remembered for the virtue they displayed—Alfonso the Kind and Richard the Lionheart, for instance. If you could choose one virtue that you would like to be remembered for, what would it be? Write your name and the virtue you would like to have in your notebook. For example, "Jill the Compassionate." What are some practical things you could to do acquire that virtue? There is a list of virtues on page 263.

WEEK 1 ~ DAY 5

A Brave Little Girl
By Mara L. Pratt, 1889

During the American Revolution, the people of Boston were suffering greatly from lack of food. The British under General Gage held the town, and the large number of British soldiers greatly depleted the amount of food in the city. In the villages around Boston, the brave patriots saw the affliction of their friends in Boston and made plans to send them food.

In a little town called Windham there was a patriotic parson named White, and he urged his people to give all they could. His little daughter, catching the spirit of loyalty, wondered how she could help the suffering Bostonians.

Soon after, the villagers prepared to send Frederic Manning to Boston with sheep and cattle and a load of wheat. The little girl thought of her pet lamb. Could she, ought she, to part with it? Running to her father, she eagerly asked his advice. But the parson, smiling kindly, said, "No, dear, it is not necessary that your little heart be tried by this bitter strife," and he bade her run away and be happy.

Still, the thought would not leave her. There in Boston were little girls, no older than herself, crying for food and clothing. She must give all she could to help them.

At last the day came on which the cattle and supplies were to be driven to town. Choking down her sobs, the little martyr untied her pet from the old apple tree, and crossing the fields, waited for Manning, the driver, at the crossroads.

"Please, sir," said she, her lip quivering and the tears rolling down her cheeks, "I want to do something for the poor starving people in Boston—I want to do my part, but I have nothing but this one little lamb. Please, sir, take it to Boston with you, but, couldn't you carry it in your arms part of the way—'cause it—it—it is so little, sir?"

Then, bursting into tears and throwing her apron over her eyes as if to shut out the sight of her dear little pet, she ran away toward her home. She was too young to understand the reason for the suffering in Boston, but she did understand that there were people who were hungry. What a selfless thing she did in sharing her one true possession with others who needed it.

Virtue Study

Recite Proverbs 31:10, the memory verse for this week.

1. Why were the people in Boston starving?
2. Why did the little girl want to help?
3. What virtues did the little girl in the story have?

What do these verses say about giving?
- ♥ Luke 6:38
- ♥ Acts 20:35
- ♥ 2 Corinthians 9:6–11

Read 1 Corinthians 5:7b, 1 Peter 1:18–19, and Revelation 5:12. Share about how Jesus was the Lamb who was slain for us. Just as the brave little girl gave her lamb for others, God sacrificed His Son for us.

Does the little girl in this story remind you of anyone in the Bible? (Read Mark 12:41–44 for one example.)

Have you ever seen someone give something he or she valued highly? Tell about it.

WEEK 2 ~ DAY 1

Living and Dying for Jesus, Part 1
By John Hunt, 1885

"Mistress, why do you not worship the gods?" enquired a young slave girl named Blandina, who lived in the second century after Christ in the city of Lyons.

The Roman lady smiled at the question. "What would it benefit me," she answered in a low, sweet voice, "to make a sacrifice to images of marble and stone?"

"But the images are merely representations of the beings which control our destinies, I believe," replied the girl, a little puzzled—"at least, so the priests tell us."

"That cannot be, Blandina," said the noble lady, "for there are no such gods as Jupiter, Mars, Venus, and the others. The images you worship are the works of men's hands, the reflections of figures which their imaginations create. The names which they bear are also given by man, and the deeds which they are said to have done are but the invention of their makers. I could not, I dare not, represent my God by any image, or presume to ascribe to His Divine Majesty such qualities as our people give to their idols."

"Ah!" exclaimed Blandina, "then you have a God?"

"Certainly," replied the lady, smiling, "a God who created all things."

"Where is He?" asked Blandina.

"Everywhere," answered her mistress. "In this room while we are speaking, in the heavens, upon the earth." And taking from under the pillow upon which she had been resting her head a roll of parchment, she bade Blandina seat herself at her feet and hear something of the God who was in all places, and yet had no image.

Blandina did as she was asked, and listened with interest and astonishment to the story of the Cross.

When it was finished she sat speechless, with the tears falling from her eyes. It seemed incredible to the clever but unschooled girl that a slave like herself, a creature whom men scorned, who possessed no rights, who had no prospect in life but years of cruel bondage, no hope in the future but the dark grave, was, notwithstanding the apparent contradictions of her lot, one whom her Creator loved, for whom Christ had died and for whom there was prepared equally with her master an eternity of joy and peace with which all the sufferings of life were not worthy to be compared.

"Can it be true?" murmured Blandina when she had recovered from her emotion.

"It is true indeed," answered her mistress, resting her hand kindly upon the bowed head, "and if you can once be made, through God's grace, to *feel* that it is, you will never bow down to images of wood and stone again."

Blandina lifted the hand of her mistress and kissed it reverently. "I will never worship the gods of my fathers again," said she in a low voice. "Henceforth, beloved lady and mistress, your God shall be mine, for if His worshipers can become so gentle and gracious in their behavior to those who are despised among men, He must indeed be worthy of devotion."

Virtue Study

Memory Verse: Hebrews 11:1. Write this verse on a 3 x 5 card and memorize.

1. What made Blandina interested in the religion of her mistress?
2. If her mistress had been cruel, would Blandina have listened to what she said about Jesus? Why or why not?
3. How can we be like Blandina's mistress?

Read the Parable of the Sower in Luke 8:5–15 and answer these questions:
- ♥ How many kinds of soil are there?
- ♥ What do each of the different kinds of soil represent?
- ♥ What kind of soil was Blandina?
- ♥ What kind of soil are you?

WEEK 2 ~ DAY 2

Living and Dying for Jesus, Part 2
By John Hunt, 1885

Blandina kept her word. Days and months passed away, and her Christian mistress did not hear of her making any offering to the false gods at the neighboring temples. She therefore took her by the hand, as a young sister eager to learn the truth, and introduced her to an assembly of Christians who met secretly in a tomb. Now Blandina heard more fully from the brethren how Jesus had died for the despised slave—suffering the death of a condemned slave to obtain freedom for all human beings who believe.

Transported with joy at the hope of salvation and a future life, she folded her hands and raised her sweet, clear voice in a hymn of thanksgiving, declaring that she should now be ready to leave the world at any moment, for all her fears had been crushed beneath the heel of the Savior.

Little did Blandina think how soon she would be required to prove her words. Only a few days passed before her mistress, whose light was not one to be hidden under a bushel, was seized and carried before the governor—charged with the crime of being a Christian. This took place during the persecution under Marcus Aurelius in AD 177.

Blandina followed weeping, and before they reached the judgment hall, the poor slave girl had been arrested also.

The circumstance added greatly to the burden which had been cast upon the shoulders of Blandina's noble Christian mistress, for the bondmaiden was but young and of a delicate disposition. She trembled with anxiety lest the fiery trial should be too great for the young girl. But God was pleased to show in this case, as in many others, how the strength that He supplies is made perfect in weakness.

In vain her executioners applied every torture. From morning till night they applied the whip, tore her flesh with sharp hooks, and burnt her with hot irons, till at last her very torturers confessed themselves conquered and were overwhelmed with amazement that she still lived. All through her agonizing sufferings she kept repeating, "I am a Christian, I am a Christian. No iniquity is committed among us"—expressions which seemed to give her superhuman strength. And when at last she was exposed to the wild beasts, and stood with her mangled form facing the shouting, yelling crowd in full view of the howling lions, a calm, sweet smile rested upon her countenance. The mouth of the lion was unto her the door of heaven, and silent as a statue, with her eyes fixed above, where her help came from, she awaited with resignation and without fear the moment when the Lord should bid her enter.

But the lions seemed awed by her courageous, majestic bearing, and they withdrew, crouching, into a corner, whence neither blows nor alarms could drive them upon the victim. The wicked, fanatic multitude, therefore, more cruel than they, and infuriated at being thwarted in their design, caused her to be enclosed in a net and set upon by a wild bull.

The wild bull, however, was as reluctant to attack Blandina as the other animals had been, and the hands of her cruel persecutors were at length obliged to release her from her agony. Her good fight fought and her sufferings ended, she passed through the dark valley of the shadow of death into the golden city, where mistress and slave were again united, nevermore to part.

Virtue Study

Work on Hebrews 11:1, the memory verse for this week.

1. How did Blandina keep the faith?
2. What did she endure for her faith?
3. What are some of the virtues mentioned in this chapter?

What do these verses say about perseverance?
- ♥ John 16:33
- ♥ Romans 5:3–5
- ♥ Hebrews 10:32–36

What does 2 Corinthians 12:9–10 say about God's strength?

In our country, we enjoy freedom to worship God! Other Christians do not have this liberty. Take a few minutes to pray for Christians who are being persecuted today.

Christians in the second century let their light shine so brightly that it was easy to find them. If you were accused of being a Christian, would there be enough evidence to convict you?

What are the characteristics of a true Christian?

WEEK 2 ~ DAY 3

The Heroine of Fort Henry, Part 1
By Mr. Blaisdell and Mr. Ball, 1905

It was near sunset of a lovely day in September during the first year of the Revolution. A scout had run into a little pioneer settlement to warn the pioneers of a coming Indian attack.

Before dark, every man, woman, and child near the settlement was safe within the stockade at Fort Henry. On the same night, down the valley of the Ohio River could be seen the flames of burning log cabins.

At sunrise Captain Mason led out a few men to look for Indians. The enemy was hiding in the corn and underbrush. They fell suddenly on the little scouting party and killed more than half of them.

Captain Ogle and twelve riflemen hurried to the help of Captain Mason. Only four men got back to the fort. The big gate was hardly shut and bolted when a hundred Indians with fierce war whoops made a dash for the stockade.

Inside the log fence, fifty women and children were huddled together, with fewer than twenty men and boys to defend them.

But three of the men were fearless fighters: Colonel Sheppard and Captains Ebenezer and Silas Zane.

Suddenly the war whoops stopped. A man named Simon Girty came toward the fort, waving a white flag.

"Surrender," he cried with an oath. "I have four hundred Indians here in the woods. A word from me, and they will kill every one of you before sunset."

"Surrender to a traitor! No, indeed," shouted Colonel Sheppard. "There may be forty of you to one of us. We will fight while there is one of us left."

Girty swore another oath, shook his fist at the fort, and went back to his Indian friends. The settlers of Fort Henry had good reason to dislike Simon Girty. When but a small boy, he had been captured by the Indians and adopted. He turned traitor to his own people and often led the Indians against the remote settlements. His name was a terror to the pioneers along the Ohio River.

When the men in Fort Henry refused to surrender, he began an attack. The fight went on for several hours, but the little garrison did not lose heart. Even the boys used their rifles with deadly effect. Some of the women molded the bullets; others cooled the guns and loaded them.

During the day, the Indians tried several times to storm the fort or set it on fire. At sunset they went into the woods, but after a time they came back and made the night hideous with their yells. All those dreadful hours, without food or sleep, the men and women stood at their posts.

At sunrise, the battle began again. At one time the Indians used logs as battering rams and tried to break down the big gate. About noon, the deadly fire of the pioneers drove the Indians into the woods, but soon the men began to whisper to each other. What was the matter?

A boy ran to his mother and cried, "Oh, Mother, the powder is almost gone!"

A rifleman at one of the loopholes turned round and said, "There are not half a dozen rounds left."

"Keep up your courage, men," shouted Captain Ebenezer Zane. "There is a keg of powder in my cabin."

But his cabin was outside the stockade, three hundred feet away.

"If we give up the fort," added Captain Silas Zane, "every man of us will be burnt at the stake, and our women and children will be carried away to Canada or put to a cruel death."

"This is no time to talk," said Colonel Sheppard. "There is a keg of powder in Captain Zane's cabin. Who will go for it?"

"I will go for it. Let me go," shouted every man and boy in that little band of pioneers.

At this moment, a young girl named Elizabeth Zane—or Betty, as she was usually called—ran up to the men and cried out, "No, no, we cannot spare a man. I will go myself. I shall not be missed. I'm not afraid. God will protect me."

Virtue Study

Work on Hebrews 11:1, the memory verse for this week.

1. What terrible situation were the pioneers facing?
2. What needed to be done?
3. How did Elizabeth Zane take the initiative?
4. Who did she trust to protect her?
5. What virtues did her actions show?

Read Psalm 3. What does this passage say about trusting in God?

What do these verses say about where our trust should be?
- Psalm 9:10
- Psalm 13:5
- Psalm 22:4
- Psalm 62:8

WEEK 2 ~ DAY 4

The Heroine of Fort Henry, Part 2
By Mr. Blaisdell and Mr. Ball, 1905

"Betty, you are only a girl," said a boy. "You can't run fast enough. The Indians will catch you."

"Never mind," replied Betty, "I'm going for the powder. Let somebody pin up my hair so that the Indians can't catch hold of it."

There was no time to lose. Even now the Indians were seen creeping out of the underbrush.

Kneeling for a moment in prayer, the young girl rose with a smile on her sweet face and said quietly, "I am ready."

The big gate of the fort was opened just wide enough for her to slip out. Slowly, as if going to pick flowers in the woods, she walked across the open space between the stockade and her brother's cabin.

For once, the Indians were off their guard. They were surprised to see a young bareheaded girl come quietly out of the fort as if for a walk.

"Squaw, squaw," the warriors shouted, but did not fire a shot.

She reached the cabin and found the powder. She stood for a moment in the doorway with the keg clasped in her arms. She gave a quick look at the big gate. It seemed a long way off.

The people in the fort watched every movement and saw her dart away toward the gate.

The Indians were not caught napping this time. Now they knew what the girl was doing. They set up a fearful yell.

Bang! Bang! cracked the rifles of the Indians. The bullets whizzed past her, but not one found its mark. Almost at the gate, she tripped and fell. *Crack! Crack!* went the bullets.

"My poor sister!" cried Silas Zane. "A bullet has hit her."

But Betty, unhurt, picked herself up and hurried on. A moment later, the big gate swung open, and the brave girl with her prize fell into the arms of her brother Silas.

Wild cheers filled Fort Henry when the defenders knew that the girl was safe.

That night, a famous pioneer arrived with fourteen men and fought his way into the stockade. At daybreak, McCulloch, another frontier hero, came with forty riflemen from neighboring settlements.

Girty now gave up the siege. After killing several hundred head of cattle and burning a few log cabins, the despised outlaw and his band hurried across the Ohio River.

The defense of Fort Henry was one of the most remarkable in the history of the frontier. Not a man of the garrison was lost during the siege. Nearly one hundred of the Indians were killed.

Twenty years later, Captain Ebenezer Zane founded the town of Zanesville in Ohio.

As for Betty Zane, she lived to a good old age, loved and respected by all who knew her. She spent all her long life near Wheeling, not far from the scene of her daring exploit.

She was often asked to tell how she got the keg of powder, but, as one young girl said who heard her tell the story, "Never did Elizabeth Zane speak of her deed boastfully or as a wonderful matter."

Virtue Study

Work on Hebrews 11:1, the memory verse for this week.

1. What did Elizabeth do before she left the fort?
2. What does that show about her character?

What do these verses say about prayer?
- Psalm 6:9
- Psalm 66:18–20
- Psalm 143:1
- Matthew 11:24
- John 17:15
- 1 Thessalonians 5:17
- Romans 12:12
- Philippians 4:6
- Colossians 4:2

When you have a decision to make or a difficult task to perform, how could you follow the example of Elizabeth Zane? What are some everyday events or circumstances you face which might go better if you prayed first? Ask someone to hold you accountable to pray more about these events.

WEEK 2 ~ DAY 5

Thwarting the British
By Mr. Blaisdell and Mr. Ball, 1917

Off the southeast coast of Massachusetts there is an island called Martha's Vineyard. On the island is the little village of Vineyard Haven.

During the war for freedom from England, the people on the island were sturdy patriots. Shortly after the battle of Lexington, the leading men of the village sent to Maine and bought a big pine tree for a flagpole. They raised the pole on a little hill just outside the village.

There was a lively time in the little seaport town when the flag was first unfurled. A few old soldiers marched to the hill. The young men with their fife and drum played the stirring and patriotic tune of the day, "The White Cockade and the Peacock's Feather." Children were in the procession too, dressed in their Sunday clothes with their hands full of flowers.

The flagpole had been there only a few weeks when the British frigate *Vixen* came sailing into the harbor. She had lost a mast in a storm, and she came into Vineyard Haven in search of a new one. The first officer, Lieutenant Dix, landed with a boat full of men.

"We are bound for Charleston," said the lieutenant, "and we need that flagpole for a mast. We can pay you well for it. If you will not sell it, we shall have to take it by force."

What could the people do? Only a few old men and sailors were left in the village. Most of the young men were at Boston, in Washington's army. Besides, the officer would pay a good price in gold. So it was voted to sell the flagpole.

"Very well," said Lieutenant Dix, "here is your money. My ship carpenters will come ashore in the morning."

When Grandfather Daggett came home to dinner that day and told the family what had happened, the women were greatly excited about it. Polly Daggett, the granddaughter, a sturdy young patriot of sixteen, was very angry.

"That British officer shall never have our flagpole if I can help it," she cried, and her black eyes flashed.

Now Polly Daggett was a smart girl. She ran across the beach to have a talk with her two friends, Bessie Nickerson and Nancy Freeman. That afternoon, the three girls had a secret meeting in an old whaleboat by the wharf.

"There is a big auger in Grandpa's boathouse," said Polly, "but what shall we do for powder?"

"Father has his big powder horn full of powder in the closet near the fireplace," replied Bessie Nickerson. "I can easily get it."

"Now, Nancy," said Polly, "see if you can find some wadding and some candlewicks for a fuse."

"All right, Polly. Mother made candles last week, and there are a few wicks left. I will bring them."

Shortly after dark, the three girls took a shortcut through the fields and across the sand dunes to the hilltop. Polly was a strong girl and knew how to use the auger. She bored three holes into the pine flagpole. Then, with a pewter spoon she filled each hole with powder, put in the wicks for a fuse, and with a piece of a broomstick rammed down the wadding. At last all was ready.

Halfway down the hill lived an old lady, Aunt Deborah Baker. Polly and Aunt Deborah were good friends, and the girls had told her their secret.

Polly now ran down the hill to Aunt Deborah's cottage and came back with a little iron kettle full of live coals. She quickly lighted the wicks and cried to her companions, "Now then, girls, run for Aunt Deborah's as fast as you can."

She seized her iron kettle, and all three girls took to their heels. A moment later, out of breath and much excited, they were seated before the great fireplace in Aunt Deborah's kitchen.

They didn't wait long. *Bang! Bang! Bang!* went the three blasts.

The people afterward said that every house in the village seemed to shake. At all events, the explosion splintered the flagpole and ruined it. The British came the next day for the new mast. The captain of the warship was angry to find the flagpole in splinters. Lieutenant Dix came ashore.

The town fathers told him that some of the bad boys in the village must have destroyed the pole. Of course they tried to find out who had played such a trick, but they could not learn anything about it. Aunt Deborah said nothing, but quietly smiled. The British frigate sailed for New York.

The three girls kept their secret for several years. Not until the war was over did they tell the story of how they had prevented the British officers from using their beloved flagpole for a mast.

Virtue Study

Recite Hebrews 11:1, the memory verse for this week.

1. Why did Polly want to destroy the flagpole?
2. How did she show initiative and resolve?
3. What are some of the virtues that Polly and her friends displayed?

What does this verse say about being discreet?
- ♥ Proverbs 2:11

Read Proverbs 8:10–12. What virtues are mentioned, and how are they connected?

In Jesus's time there was a woman who tried to be discreet about being healed. She longed to be healed but didn't want others to know about it. In the end, she *was* healed, and she had the privilege of speaking to Jesus. Read Luke 8:42–48 and Matthew 9:20–22, and answer these questions:
- ♥ Why did she touch Jesus?
- ♥ What happened to her?
- ♥ What did Jesus tell her?

Box of Visual Reminders

In your box, put an American flag. Whenever you see it, remind yourself of Polly and her quick thinking, to help the Americans and consider how we need to be prepared and discreet.

WEEK 3 ~ DAY 1

Mary Slessor, a Dundee Factory Girl
By Katharine S. Cronk and Elsie Singmaster, 1921

The night was gloomy and rain threatened, yet there were many boys and girls on Queen Street in Dundee. They were doing nothing in particular; they did not seem to be on their way anywhere. They were simply hanging about.

Opening into Queen Street were courts called *pends.* These were not streets—for they were very narrow—or thoroughfares—because they led nowhere. They were merely hallways to tall buildings where human beings huddled together like animals. They were paved with rough stones, and in order to reach the spiral staircase on the outside of the old tenements, one had to step through masses of filth.

Even so, these boys and girls found the pends and the street itself a pleasant change from the crowded rooms in which they lived. All day they worked in factories, and in the evening they naturally tried to find entertainment.

This evening they were in a good humor. They looked down the street eagerly as one might look for the approach of a circus. Presently they drew near together before the door of a little room on Queen Street. The window shades were lifted, and within were to be seen rows of benches and a little table. They looked in and laughed.

"We'll get her!" said a rough voice. "Just wait till she comes to her prayer meeting!"

"She wants to go out to Africa to teach black people!" said another, and there were shrieks of laughter as though this were the strangest wish in the world.

"Black people!" repeated the largest boy. "I'll black her eye." As he spoke, he swung a heavy object at the end of a string. It looked like a piece of lead and was a dangerous weapon.

"She's coming!" shouted a girl. "She's coming!"

There was delighted laughter and a sudden stooping to the earth. There were loose stones on Queen Street, and there was also mud—both soft, sticky mud and hard, dried mud.

"We'll get her!" cried another girl.

"We'll make her let us alone."

A foe worthy of these numerous and fierce opponents should have been tall and strong and well-armed, but the approaching figure was that of a girl. Her name was Mary Slessor; she was fourteen years old and short for her age. She had not had a chance to grow to her full height because she got up at five o'clock in the morning, helped her mother until she

THE "PENDS"

went to the factory at six, worked twelve hours, and then helped her mother until bedtime. When she had a spare moment she read, even propping her book up on her loom as the great missionary Livingstone had done when he was a factory boy.

The shouts of the boys and girls grew louder. "Hi, Mary Slessor!" said one. "Hit her!" chimed in another.

The little figure came straight on.

"We're not going to come to your meetings!" shouted a loud voice.

"We don't care for your meetings!" yelled another.

"You clear right out of here!" howled a third.

Still the little figure advanced. "I won't give up," she shouted back, white-faced and stubborn. "You can do what you like, I won't give up!"

In answer to this defiance there was a moment's silence. Then the largest boy stepped out with his weight tied to a cord in his hand. "All right," he said. "Then look out for your head!" His companions moved back out of danger, and he began to swing the lead round and round.

"You can't frighten me," said Mary. "I'm going to go to the meetings, and I'm going to invite you to the meetings. You can't stop me."

She stood perfectly still. The tall boy moved nearer. He lifted his arm and began to swing the piece of lead round and round in the air. It passed within six inches of Mary's face; another swing, and it was within four inches. Now it touched a flying wisp of her hair. Another swing and it might kill her. But the boy dropped his arm and let the cruel weapon fall. For the first time in his unruly life he had been beaten—not by force, but by love. "Let her alone," he said gruffly. "She's game."

A little color came into Mary's pale cheeks. Most persons would have been satisfied with this victory, but Mary was not. She boldly repeated the crime for which she had been so nearly punished.

"Will you come to my meeting?" she asked.

The leader put both hands into his pockets. "Well, this beats me!" he said. His companions expected that now Mary Slessor's hour had come. Instead, he turned on them furiously.

"Go on in!" he commanded, and into the meeting they went.

Virtue Study

Memory Verse: Philippians 2:14–15. Write this verse on a 3 x 5 card and memorize it during the week.

1. Why did those young people want to harm Mary?
2. What was her crime?
3. How did she show her trust in God?
4. If she had been injured, would she still have followed Christ?

What do these verses say about trust?
- Psalm 20:7
- Psalm 37:5–6
- Psalm 56:3–4
- Proverbs 3:5–6
- Isaiah 26:4
- Daniel 3:28

Does this story remind you of a Bible story where someone was willing to stand up for God no matter what the cost? (Read Daniel 3 for an example.)

WEEK 3 ~ DAY 2

Mary Slessor the Missionary, Part 1
By Katharine S. Cronk and Elsie Singmaster, 1921

Deep in Africa there was a stir in the woods. Dawn was not yet complete, though there was a grayish light over everything and a pink glow in the eastern sky. The trees were tall, the foliage dark, and here and there were gorgeous flowers. Now and then a parrot or a monkey chattered high up on the branches.

So far everything was beautiful. But in the deep thickets there were sounds which were not beautiful, the angry shouts of harsh, human voices. Advancing through the bushes were many black men, wearing almost no clothing but armed to the teeth. They carried knives in their belts and spears and guns in their hands. Their black eyes glittered, and their teeth gleamed. They were on the warpath, and they looked as terrible as charging beasts of prey. They were a tribe of the Okoyong country, going to meet another tribe in battle, a member of which had injured their chief. Nothing could stop them from going.

Suddenly, they heard the sound of advancing footsteps and a shrill call. They tightened their grasp on their weapons. Was the enemy at hand? Then up and at him!

But it was not an enemy. The voice was not that of a warrior, it was that of a woman. It was not even that of an Okoyong woman, it was that of a white woman. "Stop!" it called, in the language of the Okoyong. "Stop! Listen to me!"

There came into view a little woman who looked, in spite of the passing of many years, like the girl who had defied the boys in Queen Street. She was not much taller and certainly no stouter. Her hair was cut short, and this made her look much as she had long ago. It was undoubtedly Mary Slessor.

She advanced rapidly, running over the ground in bare feet. One could not keep one's shoes dry in the damp grass, and it was better to go without shoes.

"Stop!" she called again. "Listen to me!"

"Ma is coming!" said a dozen angry voices.

"She needn't think she can stop us with any of her peace talk!"

"Disgrace has been put upon us," said another. "We must have vengeance."

The warriors shook their heads impatiently. They would listen, but they would not obey. The little figure came nearer and nearer and stood looking at them.

Calabar was not only one of the most beautiful places in the world, it was one of the most terrible. Just as into the pends of Dundee had crowded all the poor and wretched beings who could not afford to live elsewhere, so into Calabar Africa had drifted the most ignorant, the most degraded, the most persecuted of the black men on the west coast. From the sea came a terrible enemy, the slave trader. The country was under the control of England, but no white men penetrated it to face death from starvation, fever, or the bullet or poisoned arrow or spear tip of a warrior.

Missionaries try to speak as kindly as possible about the people among whom they work, but for these poor Africans they had only dreadful words: "bloody," "savage," "cruel," "crafty," "devilish," "murderers." They did their best for them along the coast, but their efforts to penetrate inland were in vain. It was no wonder they were "bloody," "savage," and "cruel," since the white man whom the Africans knew was a thief who stole men, who taught them new ways of murdering one another, and who brought them rum which made beasts of them.

Most fierce and terrible of all the tribes and most dangerous to the white man were the Okoyong, whose watchword seemed to be "war." They fought among themselves in their own villages and in various tribes, but most of all they fought the surrounding nations.

Into this country Mary Slessor had gone, and here she was at dawn, alone, facing a tribe of angry men—not only facing them, but giving them orders.

She had left Scotland and lived for a while in the mission school at Duke Town, near the coast where all was orderly, and there had learned the language. Now she lived in a mud hut and ate the food of the natives, partly so that she might have a large share of her salary to send home to her mother, and partly because she wanted to learn the hearts of the native men and women and the secrets of their dreadful customs. If she knew why they believed it necessary to kill the wives of a chief when he died and put their bodies with his into the grave, if she knew why they threw poor little twin babies into the bushes to die, if she knew why they offered human sacrifices, then she might be able to persuade them to understand their own wickedness.

Virtue Study

Work on Philippians 2:14–15, the memory verse for this week.

1. How did Mary serve God before she went to Calabar? (Look at yesterday's chapter if you can't remember.)
2. Why was the Okoyong tribe going to war?
3. How did Mary try to become one of the tribe in order to minister to them?

What does this verse say about how to reach people who need Jesus?
- ♥ 1 Corinthians 9:19–23

Mary Slessor had a lot of courage, but her boldness came from God. What do these verses say about pressing on in the face of hardship?
- ♥ 2 Corinthians 4:1
- ♥ 2 Corinthians 4:8–10
- ♥ 2 Corinthians 4:16–18

What do these verses say about being bold?
- ♥ Psalm 138:3
- ♥ Proverbs 28:1
- ♥ 1 Corinthians 3:12

WEEK 3 ~ DAY 3

Mary Slessor the Missionary, Part 2
By Katharine S. Cronk and Elsie Singmaster, 1921

Mary Slessor asked at last to be sent to Okoyong, and here she was without white companionship, but with many black companions. She had even adopted a family, all of them black. One was a little girl, brought to her by a white trader.

"I found this tiny baby thing in the bush," he said. "It is a twin, and the other is dead."

Mary called the baby Janie, for her sister in Scotland. Finally she had seven, who would otherwise have died and whom she nursed and taught and trained.

The Okoyong, those who would not have endured the presence of a man, tolerated her. She lived at first in the king's hut, where they were able to watch her day and night. They believed that she could do them no harm, and they were willing to let her prescribe for their illnesses and try to heal their poor bodies. They called her "Ma," and when she did not oppose their customs, they obeyed her.

Mary Slessor was not one to tolerate evil or to step aside from a path which she had set for herself. When human sacrifices were to be offered after the death of a young chief, she grew frantic. She mocked and commanded and even slept beside the prisoners so that they should not be murdered, and she helped them escape. She was a peacemaker, and she proved the witch doctors to be impostors. Day in and day out, she preached of a Kingdom of Love until the natives began to understand what it would be to live at peace with their fellows, to be free from fear and superstition, and to have hope in God.

The government sent no consul into the district but appointed Mary Slessor instead, and she sat in distant villages and heard disagreements and debated with great chiefs about proper punishment for criminals, about trade, and about matters in dispute between the natives and the government. She was called "The White Queen of Okoyong."

Now she was growing old, and her little body was racked by fever. She was often so tired that she did not see how she could live, but she saw her work prospering. It was necessary for her to have a rest, and she was about to leave. She was packing her few belongings, and the river steamer was almost at hand.

At the last minute, someone brought her a message. A chief had been injured by a man from another tribe, and his own tribesmen were on their way to avenge him.

She did not hesitate for an instant, unless it was to look at a picture which hung on the wall of her little hut. It was the likeness of the young man who had once defied her in Queen Street in Dundee. From the moment when he had entered her meeting, he had led a better life, and he had

MARY SLESSOR'S HOUSE

sent her his picture and that of his wife and children to show her how prosperous they were. With the recollection of that courageous stand in her mind, she set out on her journey. She might miss the boat and not get home, but that made no difference. How could she rest if she knew that behind her all her work was being undone?

The chief men of the village opposed her going. "They will kill you. They are mad; they will shoot wildly. If you are not assassinated, you will be shot by accident."

Undaunted, Mary shook her head and started, a man going before her beating a drum to show that a free and protected person was coming. She marched straight to the village, but there the warriors deceived her. They said they would call her in the morning that she might go with them. They called her as they had promised, but not until they were ready to start. By the time she had quickly sprung up from the earth where she was sleeping, the warriors were off.

They showed great folly, however, when they believed that they could get rid of Mary Slessor. A hundred yards away she caught up to them, and now she stood calling to them, "Stop! Listen!" Mary looked at them scornfully. She knew how to talk to them. "Don't carry on like small boys! Be quiet."

To their amazement, she walked straight through their ranks and on to the village where the enemy was drawn up in battle array.

"I salute you," she said.

The enemy was too much astonished and enraged to answer.

"Where are your manners?" she said with gentle reproach. She began to smile and joke.

At once, an old man stepped out and knelt down at her feet. Here was one person at least with manners.

"Once when I was sick, you came to see me and healed me. This is a foolish quarrel. We beg you to make peace for us."

"You bring three men," she commanded, "and three men will come from the other side, and we will have a conference."

For hours she listened to their story. She coaxed them and commanded them and pleaded with them and laughed at them. In the end she conquered, and they made peace. Then she said a few simple words about her Savior and went back over the dark, lonely forest path. The boat had gone, but messengers were waiting to take her down the river in a canoe.

Virtue Study

Work on Philippians 2:14–15, the memory verse for this week.

1. How did Mary set aside her own needs to give to others?
2. How did Mary display the gift of being a peacemaker?

What do these verses say about peacemaking?
- ♥ Matthew 5:9
- ♥ James 3:17–18
- ♥ Romans 14:17–19

There are several people in the Bible who were peacemakers. Can you think of any of them? (Read 1 Samuel 25 and Acts 9:26–30 for some examples.)

How can you become a peacemaker in your own home?

Mary was faithful in all she did. What does Matthew 25:14–30 say about faithfulness?

WEEK 3 ~ DAY 4

Mary Slessor of Calabar

By Katharine S. Cronk and Elsie Singmaster, 1921

The afternoon was pleasant at Duke Town, along the coast of Calabar. Some great event seemed about to happen. The chief missionary, Mr. MacGregor, was moving about busily, now in the missionary buildings, now in his own house. The governor-general and the commissioner sat on their porches, looking out as though they were watching for something or somebody, or waiting for something to begin. When Europeans met, they stopped and said a pleasant word to one another.

It was more than thirty years since Mary Slessor had landed in Duke Town, and there were many changes. The government buildings were larger and finer, the mission buildings had increased in number and size, and there were many other improvements. England had begun to busy herself with the affairs of her colony, and the church at home was listening to the desperate call from Calabar.

Presently, a long line of boys appeared from the boys' school and filed into the hall of the mission buildings. Then there came an equally long file from the girls' school. At once, the chief missionary and the other missionaries and the governor-general and the commissioner went there also, followed by the Europeans and the natives.

They took their assigned places on the platform and the benches and sat waiting. They watched the door even as the naughty boys and girls had looked up the street in Dundee, and as the Okoyong chiefs had looked out from between the branches.

"She's coming!" said a whisper. The whisper passed all along the benches. "She's coming! She's coming!"

A little figure advanced to the platform, hesitated, and moved on, assisted by firm and tender hands and urged by laughing voices.

"Now, come along, Ma! Are you afraid, Ma?"

It must be confessed that Mary Slessor was afraid. Afraid of all these eyes, though she was accustomed to facing thousands of eyes set in black faces; afraid of all these smiles, though she was accustomed to friendliness. Most of all, she was afraid of what was being said. Almost before she was seated, the commissioner began to speak.

"Miss Slessor, I have in my hand a box which contains a silver badge of the Order of the Hospital of St. John of Jerusalem in England, of which the king is the sovereign head. This badge is conferred only on persons professing the Christian faith who are eminently distinguished for philanthropy. It is a Maltese cross, embellished in the angles by lions and unicorns. I have been directed by the king to bestow this badge upon you in recognition of your service to the government. You have opened the country of Okoyong. You, above all others, have been instrumental in preserving peace. You have let in a great light where there was darkness, and England thanks you, her only woman consul."

Mary not only was afraid, but she looked afraid. Her head bent lower and lower; her hands were lifted to hide her face. But at last she had to rise and have the medal pinned on her shoulder. She stood for a moment, trembling, then looked down at the pleased, attentive faces. She saw herself a little girl in Scotland and then a woman in Africa, and once again she grew calm and brave and even a little ashamed of her embarrassment. The credit for what she had done was not hers. She would tell where it belonged, and then she would feel comfortable.

"If I have done anything in my life," she said, "it has been easy, because the Master has gone before."

Then she sat down neither proud nor afraid, but content.

Virtue Study

Work on Philippians 2:14–15, the memory verse for this week.

1. What does the phrase "eminently distinguished for philanthropy" mean?
2. Even brave people like Mary Slessor have things they are afraid of. Why was Mary afraid?
3. How did she overcome her fear?

What do these verses say about fear?
- Isaiah 41:10
- Isaiah 43:1–2
- 2 Timothy 1:7
- 1 John 4:18

Mary Slessor once said, "Blessed the man and woman who is able to serve cheerfully in the second rank—a big test." How did her life show that she was willing to serve unnoticed? What are some second-rank jobs that you could do for others? Do one of them today.

Fear and worry often go hand in hand. What does Matthew 6:25–34 say about worry?

Box of Visual Reminders

Put a stone in your box. The bad young people of Dundee tried to frighten Mary with stones, but Mary wasn't frightened. She had learned to lean on the Rock of Ages. When you see this rock in the box, think about how God is your Rock.

WEEK 3 ~ DAY 5

Two Girls Who Braved the Sea
By Samuel Smiles, 1900

Along the coast of western Australia, a gentlewoman named Grace Vernon Bussell rode on her noble horse. She glanced out into the stormy sea and saw the steamer *Georgette* stranded on the shore near Perth. A lifeboat had escaped from the boat with the women and children on board, but it was swamped by the surf, which was running very high. The poor creatures were all struggling in the water, clinging to the boat, and in imminent peril of their lives when, on the top of a steep cliff, appeared a young lady on horseback.

Wind in her hair, her first thought was how to save these drowning women and children. She galloped down the cliff—how, it is impossible to say—urged her horse into the surf, and beyond the second line of the breakers, she reached the boat. She succeeded in bringing the women and children on shore. There was still a man left, and she plunged into the sea again and rescued him. So fierce was the surf that four hours were occupied in landing fifty persons.

As soon as they were all on shore, the heroic lady, drenched with the sea foam and half-fainting with fatigue, galloped off to her home, twelve miles distant, to send help and relief to the rescued people on the beach. Her sister now took up the work. She went back through the woods to the shore, taking with her a provision of tea, milk, sugar, and flour. Next day, the rescued were brought to her house and cared for until they recovered enough to depart on their solitary ways. It is melancholy to have to record that Mrs. Brookman, the heroine's sister, took cold in the midst of her exertions and died of fever.

No less brave was the conduct of a young woman in the Shetlands, who went to sea to save the lives of some fishermen when no one else would volunteer to go. A violent storm had broken over the remote island of Unst when the fishing fleet—the main source of income for the inhabitants—was at sea. One by one the boats reached the haven in safety, but the last boat was still out, and it was observed by those ashore that it was in great difficulties. It capsized, and the sailors were seen struggling in the water.

At this juncture, Helen Petrie, a slender lass, stepped forward and urged that an attempt to rescue them should be made at all hazards. The men said it was certain death to those who wished to put off in such a storm.

Nevertheless, Helen Petrie was willing to brave death. She hastily stepped into a small boat. Her sister-in-law joined her, and her father, who was lame in one hand, took charge of the rudder. Two of the crew of the fishing boat had already disappeared, but two remained, clinging to the upturned keel of their craft. It was these the women went to save. After great exertions, they reached the wreck. Just as they approached it, one of the men was washed off, and he would certainly have been drowned had not Helen caught him by his hair and dragged him into the boat. The other man was also rescued, and the whole returned to the haven in safety.

Later in life, Helen Petrie became a maid, and her heroic actions were forgotten. However, when she died, people again remembered the valiant service she had rendered to those drowning men.

Virtue Study

Recite Philippians 2:14–15, the memory verse for this week.

1. How did Grace and Helen respond when they saw an emergency?
2. What does this show us about their character?

Grace and Helen were attentive to others around them and eagerly helped those who were in need. Are you attentive to those you come into contact with? Do you see when someone needs help? Share some stories of how you have helped others. What are some ways you could work on becoming more attentive?

These young ladies were also very helpful to others. What do these verses say about being helpful?
- ♥ Acts 20:35
- ♥ Ephesians 4:29
- ♥ 1 Timothy 5:9–10

Are there any Bible characters who displayed attentiveness? (An example is found in 2 Kings. Read 2 Kings 5:1–19. How did this young girl help her captors by paying attention to their needs?)

WEEK 4 ~ DAY 1

The American Army of Two
By Mr. Blaisdell and Mr. Ball, 1905

In 1812, the United States again fought a war against Great Britain. The little village of Scituate, on the coast of Massachusetts, was a great fishing place in those days. Sometimes a hundred boats ran into the harbor for shelter. Near the village lived a lighthouse keeper named Bates, whose oldest daughter was called Rebecca.

It was a fine morning in August, and Rebecca was busy polishing the lantern. Looking over the sparkling ocean, she saw a strange vessel in the bay slowly making for the shore. "That must be the British warship we heard of yesterday," thought the frightened girl.

She ran down the steep lighthouse stairs and across the yard into their cottage. "Mother," she cried, "get the glass and look! There's a big warship in plain sight!"

The lighthouse keeper had gone to the village on an errand. There was nobody at home except his wife, his two little boys, and his two daughters: Rebecca, who was about seventeen, and Abigail, who was about fifteen. Mrs. Bates watched the vessel through the spyglass. "Of course that is a British ship," she said, "and it looks as if it were making for our harbor. Run over to the village, boys, find your father, and give the alarm."

You may be sure that all the village people kept a sharp lookout on that distant ship. "That warship can sink every boat in the harbor and burn the village," said a young fisherman.

For two hours the vessel tacked and stood off to sea; then, as the tide began to flow, it made for the shore. It was high tide at two o'clock. With all her sails set, the great warship swept grandly over the bar and anchored at a point of land half a mile from the lighthouse.

The boats were lowered, and the helpless people saw the soldiers rapidly nearing the shore. What a running to and fro there was in the village! Nets, clothing, and all kinds of household goods were loaded into hay carts and hurried away behind the sand hills. The women and children hastened off to the woods.

The two sisters sat watching from the lighthouse tower. Five large boats were close to land. They were rowed by sailors in blue jackets and filled with soldiers in bright red coats. How the guns glittered! How the gold lace on the officers' uniforms sparkled!

"Oh, my!" said Rebecca. "I wish I could take Father's old gun and help the men fight."

"I know what we'll do," cried Abigail suddenly, "let's take Father's drum and beat it. You know how to drum, Rebecca."

"That's just the thing," said the older girl. "We will take the fife in Mother's bureau drawer too. You can play that. We will hide behind the sand hills and give them 'Yankee Doodle.' Perhaps we can fool them."

The excited girls got the drum and covered it with a shawl, then they found the fife, and away they went to the outside beach. Creeping behind the low sand hills and the beach grass, out of sight of the soldiers, they sat down on the sand to tighten the drum and softly try the fife.

"We must march along the outside beach toward the lighthouse, just as if we were at the head of a regiment," said Abigail.

"Good!" answered Rebecca. "We will make them think that soldiers have come from Boston to help us fight."

Rubadub, dub! Rubadub, dub, beat Rebecca in lively fashion. *Squeak, squeak, squeak,* went Abigail's fife. This was too much for the young girls. In spite of their fears, they stopped marching and sat down on the sand to laugh.

"This will never do!" cried Rebecca. "We shall spoil everything."

"I will behave better next time," said Abigail. "Let us try again."

"Forward! March! One, two!"

Louder and louder rolled the drum, and clearer and clearer whistled the fife. Across the harbor, the men in the village were listening. "That's the soldiers from Boston coming to fight," they said.

Meanwhile, the redcoats were setting fire to a fishing sloop. The officers were amazed at the sound of the music.

"Can it be possible," one said, "that the Yankees are marching a regiment down to the point? If they have cannon with them, all our boats will be shut up in the harbor."

"The drums are coming nearer, and there is the sound of the fife. Hark! Of all tunes in the world, those impudent fellows are playing 'Yankee Doodle'! Quick, men!" cried the commander. "The Yankees will sink every boat unless we can get past that point."

There was no time to talk. It was a question of getting out of the harbor and reaching their ship. Every moment they expected a regiment to open fire upon them at close range. Soon after dark, the British man-of-war sailed away.

The two sisters had saved their village and were hailed as heroes!

Virtue Study

Memory Verse: Jeremiah 29:11. Write this verse on a 3 x 5 card and memorize it during the week.

1. What danger did Rebecca and Abigail face, and what were their actions?
2. What virtues did they display?

Rebecca and Abigail showed what can be done with very little. There are several stories in the Bible that show resourcefulness. In the book of Ruth, we find a young widow doing what she could with what she had. Read Ruth 2:2–23. How was she resourceful?

WEEK 4 ~ DAY 2

The Mother of Andrew Jackson, Part 1
By William Judson Hampton, 1922

Andrew Jackson's father, whose name was also Andrew, immigrated with his wife and two sons from Carrickfergus, Ireland, to South Carolina in 1765. Andrew's mother's name was Elizabeth Hutchinson.

Both Andrew and Elizabeth were of Scottish-Irish descent and were ardent Presbyterians. Their only source of income was their hands and an eagerness to work. They settled at Waxhaw, near the boundary line between North and South Carolina. Here Andrew built a log house, and in it he sheltered his family. The Jacksons' neighbors were few, and as poor as themselves.

When they had succeeded in clearing the land and raising one crop, the father suddenly died. He had lived in obscurity, and in obscurity he was buried. Mrs. Jackson, with her fatherless boys, rode to the graveyard in the wagon that carried her husband's rude casket to the grave. He was buried in a field, no one knows exactly where. The mother was left penniless. Mrs. Jackson went directly from the grave of her husband to the log cabin home of her sister,

66 ♥ *Heroines of the Past Bible Study*

and here, on March 15, 1767, a few days after her husband's burial, Andrew Jackson was born.

What a scene! Who would dream that a future president of the United States could possibly come out of such lowly surroundings? There was the pain-crushed, heart-stricken widow—no home of her own, a small babe, coarse fare, poverty, and wild surroundings. As her invalid sister's housekeeper, Mrs. Jackson worked hard, washing, mending, and cooking, in order to help pay for the support of herself and children. Like most women of Scottish-Irish blood, she was strong, capable, thrifty, a fine housekeeper, and a wise and affectionate mother.

Part of the first ten years of Andrew's life was spent with his Uncle Crawford on a farm. Here he learned to do the general work such as a lad of his years could perform.

In the winter, he attended a log schoolhouse located in a pine forest nearby. The support of the teacher was pledged by the responsible farmers of the neighborhood, and not much more was taught than the three Rs. Mrs. Jackson was anxious that her youngest son, who had never seen his father, should have a good education. She had fond hopes that he might someday become a Presbyterian minister.

She was very devout, and regularly and prayerfully read her Bible. She had been impressed by many striking incidents in the

Bible, where godly parents had consecrated their children to the Lord.

So in simple trust, she consecrated Andrew to the service of God. In her devout and simple faith, she believed all things and hoped all things. Her fond hopes were never to be realized. Yet because of this hope, her mother love was elevated and ennobled, and Andrew's childhood days were enveloped by a spiritual atmosphere that fairly breathed of heaven.

His nature easily responded to those religious influences. He loved and reverenced his mother with devotion. Her religious habits—praying on her knees by her bedside; her daily Bible reading; her custom of having him read the Bible; and the prayers she taught him at her knee, with a hand laid lovingly on his head—all these sacred influences entered into his soul and stayed there forever.

As the years went by and Andrew's character developed, her hopes regarding his future intensified. She toiled, scrimped, schemed, and impoverished herself in order that Andrew might be helped. But Andrew Jackson was destined not to preach the gospel of the Son of God, but the gospel of patriotism.

In his early life, Jackson drifted a long way off from the coveted desire of his mother. Possibly it was after her death. Be that as it may, he never got away from his mother's influence and prayers, and a mother's prayers were in the end answered.

Andrew was nine years old when the Declaration of Independence was signed, and fourteen when the war reached Waxhaw. The schools were closed. Andrew and his brother Robert were at home when Tarleton and his dragoons thundered along the red roads of Waxhaw and dyed them a deeper red with the blood of the surprised militia. The old meeting house at Waxhaw was speedily converted into a hospital, and here the worst cases of the hundred and fifty wounded militiamen, victims of Tarleton's dragoons, were carried.

Virtue Study

Work on Jeremiah 29:11, the memory verse for this week.

1. What did Mrs. Jackson do after the death of her husband?
2. What did she want Andrew to be?
3. What virtues did she have?

Mrs. Jackson consecrated her son to God. In the book of Samuel, we read about another mother who did the same thing. Read 1 Samuel 1 and answer these questions:
- ♥ Why was Hannah sad?
- ♥ What did she ask God to do?
- ♥ What did she promise in return?
- ♥ Did she keep her promise?
- ♥ What happened to her after she took Samuel to the temple?

WEEK 4 ~ DAY 3

The Mother of Andrew Jackson, Part 2
By William Judson Hampton, 1922

Mrs. Jackson was one of the first of the women of the settlement to turn in and help lessen the distress of her wounded countrymen. Robert and Andrew were among the young patriots who volunteered to ward off the Tories at Waxhaw. Both were taken prisoners. A Tory officer commanded Andrew to blacken his boots. Andrew replied, "Sir, I am a prisoner of war, and claim to be treated as such." The officer glared at him like a wild beast and aimed a desperate blow at his head. Andrew broke the force of the blow with his hand and received two wounds, a deep gash on the head and another on the hand. The scars from these he carried to his dying day.

The officer turned next to Robert and ordered him to blacken his boots. Robert saw the wounds of his brother and the fresh blood pouring from them, and he had every reason to fear a like assault in case he should refuse. But he did refuse, and the officer dealt him a terrific blow on the head, which leveled him to the floor and disabled him.

The Jackson boys, still suffering from their wounds and despairing of escape from their imprisonment, began to show symptoms of smallpox. Their mother, who had long been striving for their exchange, reached Camden with an order for their release. In exchange for thirteen British soldiers, she received her two boys,  her nephew (Thomas Crawford), and four of her Waxhaw neighbors.

When this devoted mother saw her sons, she scarcely knew them, so wasted were they with wounds, starvation, and disease. Robert could not sit on horseback unsupported. Andrew was reduced to a skeleton, but the fire of his eyes was not dimmed, nor was his dauntless spirit subdued.

Determined, if possible, to get her boys home at once, Mrs. Jackson procured two horses, one of which she rode herself, and placed her son Robert on the other. He was held in his seat by his companions. Last of all walked Andrew, without shoes, without a hat, wearing nothing but shirt and trousers, both ragged.

When these forlorn wayfarers were almost in sight of their home, a cold and driving rain set in, which chilled both of these fevered boys to their marrow. They reached home well-nigh exhausted. Two days later Robert Jackson died, and Andrew was raving in delirium. He had a narrow escape from death. After a desperate struggle, his mother's admirable nursing saved his life, but he did not fully recover for many long months.

Long before his strength returned, disturbing rumors spread through both Carolinas to the effect that hundreds of American prisoners, among them many of Mrs. Jackson's relatives and neighbors, were perishing of hunger and disease in the Charleston prison ships, a hundred and sixty miles distant. Inspired by her success in the exchange of her sons, Mrs. Jackson set out for Charleston, accompanied by two other women, with the intent to procure, if possible, the release of her friends and relatives. It is known that those noble and devoted women reached the prison-ships, carrying joy and hope to despairing men.

Andrew Jackson never saw his mother again. At the house of a relative near Charleston, she was seized with the ship-fever, of which she died after a short illness. She was buried on the open plain nearby, in an unmarked grave—a grave which Andrew Jackson could never find, though in after years he sought for it with the energy which his love and devotion inspired.

For this wise and resolute mother, Andrew Jackson cherished to his life's end a deep admiration. He loved to speak of his mother's firmness, of her good sense, of her capacity, and of her compassionate heart. He loved to quote her maxims concerning the conduct of life, especially one: "Never to injure another, nor to accept from another an injury unredressed." Often in the heat of argument, when he was at the height of his renown, he would quote some homely saying, with the remark, "That I learned from my good old mother."

How little that "good old mother" knew what the result of her maternal faithfulness was to be! How little she dreamed that, in her lowly sphere, and in her humble, pious way, she was training for a great career the hero of the age! In truth, she had imparted to her son what was of far more value than the learning of the schools, than the knowledge of commerce. From her he had learned to believe in God, in the Bible, in virtue, in the sacredness of woman's purity and love, in everything which gives strength to character, nobility to human nature, and honor and dignity to life.

Virtue Study

Work on Jeremiah 29:11, the memory verse for this week.

1. How did Mrs. Jackson take care of her sons?
2. What did she do to serve her country?
3. What virtues did she have?

Continuing the story of Hannah from yesterday, read 1 Samuel 2:1–11 and answer these questions.
- ♥ How does she begin her prayer?
- ♥ What names does she use to describe God?
- ♥ What are some of the things that God brings about?
- ♥ How does she end her prayer?

Box of Visual Reminders

Mrs. Jackson lived during the American Revolution. Print up a copy of the Declaration of Independence and put it in your box. You may find a copy online at http://www.loc.gov/rr/program/bib/ourdocs/DeclarInd.html. When you see it, remember how Mrs. Jackson instilled the love of God and country into Andrew's life.

WEEK 4 ~ DAY 4

Marcelle and the Great War
By Albert Bushnell Hart, 1920

During the First World War, the Somme District in France was the scene of much fighting. There were many brave ladies who helped fight against the Germans. French heroines were not few—indeed, to be a woman of France was to be a heroine in those slow, grinding years of the war that tired the soul as it trampled the life of that country. But none of them was of greater courage or of more resolutely self-sacrificing purpose than a young woman of Picardy, a mere girl, Marcelle Semmer. She was the daughter of a phosphate factory owner, an Alsatian who had left Alsace in 1871 rather than remain a subject of Germany.

After the defeat of the Allies at Charleroi, the French tried to make a stand along the Somme, but being unable to resist the overwhelming mass of the invaders, they fell back across a canal in the vicinity of Marcelle Semmer's home. The enemy was in close pursuit. As the last group of the French crossed the bridge, Marcelle rushed forward and, raising the drawbridge, threw the control key into the canal, without which the drawbridge could not be lowered. This remarkable evidence of presence of mind and coolness was hardly to have been expected from a girl in such terrifying circumstances.

The act was a daring one, as the advancing Germans did not hesitate to fire at her as well as at the retreating soldiers. But realizing that it would hold up the advance of the Germans, she unhesitatingly confronted the danger. It was the saving grace for the French, for it was not until the next morning that the Germans were able to get together boats enough to form a pontoon across the canal.

Though the risks were great, Marcelle remained in the village during the German occupation in order to be of possible help to the French. Indeed, she did render assistance. There was near the village of Eclusier a subterranean passage used in the working of a phosphate mine, and in this passage Marcelle managed to conceal at different times sixteen French soldiers who had been separated from their command in the retreat from Charleroi and Mons. There she fed them, furnished them with civilian clothes, and aided their escape to the French lines. It was not until she was helping the seventeenth to escape that she was caught and dragged, with the French soldier, before the local commandant.

Asked if she meant deliberately to aid the soldier to escape, she replied firmly, "Yes. He is not the first. I helped sixteen others to get away. Do what you please with me. I am not afraid to die."

With little ceremony, she was ordered to be shot. She was taken out for the purpose. The firing squad was drawn up, and only waited the order to fire when suddenly there was a roar of French artillery bombarding the town and the position of the Germans around Eclusier. It was an unexpected French advance, and without thought of the girl, the firing squad joined the confusion of men hurrying to the shelter of their defenses. Marcelle made her escape to the friendly subterranean passage. The French occupied Eclusier.

Now, the Somme lay between the opposing armies, and in the vicinity of Eclusier it forms a marshy lake. At flood the water covered the lines so that soldiers often lost their way, and here Marcelle found another means of serving France.

Being thoroughly acquainted with the neighborhood, she used to pilot parties of soldiers. Again this brought her close to death. While leading a squad of men who wanted to dig an advanced trench in the village of Frise, she fell into the hands of a party of Germans.

They locked her up in the little village church of Frise. On the morrow, she felt sure, they would shoot her.

But once more the French artillery were her salvation. The French across the Somme began a lively bombardment of Frise. One shell blew a large hole in the church wall. Through this hole, unperceived by her captors, Marcelle crawled. Creeping past the Germans scattered through Frise, she soon tumbled, safe and sound, into the nearest French trench.

By this time her fame had spread, and rewards began to shower upon her. She got the Cross of the Legion of Honor, and some time later the War-Cross. In spite of all she had gone through, she persisted in staying in the Somme country and continued to work for the cause of France. For fifteen months she remained, despite shot and shell, in her little Somme village, taking care of wounded soldiers. Also among her charges was a woman of ninety, too feeble to travel to a safer place. Marcelle looked out for her night and day with untiring devotion.

Everywhere, soldiers knew and admired her. One English general ordered his soldiers to salute when she passed and refrain from addressing her unless she spoke first. Under the strain of her volunteer work, she finally came near to a breakdown and was persuaded to go to Paris for a rest.

Virtue Study

Work on Jeremiah 29:11, the memory verse for this week.

1. How did Marcelle help her country?
2. Why was she unafraid?
3. What virtues did she display?

What do these verses say about courage?
- ♥ Deuteronomy 31:6–8
- ♥ 2 Chronicles 32:7
- ♥ Matthew 14:27
- ♥ 1 Corinthians 16:13–14
- ♥ Philippians 1:20

Read Joshua 2. How did she have the courage to save her family when the rest of her countrymen were afraid?

WEEK 4 ~ DAY 5

Felicitas, a First-Century Christian of Rome
By John Hunt, 1885

"The example of Felicitas is dangerous. She must be made to sacrifice," decided the heathen priests in their councils, and they sent a letter to the emperor to that effect.

Meanwhile Felicitas, the noble Roman widow, unconscious of the feeling she had excited, quietly lived her simple Christian life and continued to impress upon her seven sons that there was but one God, who had given His only Son, Jesus of Nazareth, to be crucified for our redemption. Such was the effect produced by her conduct and influence that many of her neighbors renounced the worship of false deities and embraced the faith of Christ.

Felicitas rejoiced over every new convert, but her time of sowing was fast passing away, and the hour for her to reap the reward of her labors was at hand.

One day when she was peacefully pursuing her ordinary activities, a party of soldiers suddenly entered her home, seized her and her sons, and carried them before Publius, who was at that time prefect or chief magistrate of Rome.

Publius was a man of some feeling, and he was sorry to see a noble lady in such a position. He therefore took Felicitas aside and tried, by means of arguments and inducements, to persuade her to deny Christ and make an offering to the gods. He was extremely unwilling to stoop to any cruelty, but to all his lectures she only answer, "Think not, Publius, to win me over by fair speeches, for the Spirit of God is within me, and will not suffer that I should be overcome by Satan, but will, I am confident, render me victorious."

Publius for a long time refused to despair of success. "Oh, unhappy woman!" he exclaimed. "Is it possible that you can think death so desirable as to force me to destroy not only yourself, but your children as well, by most dreadful torments?"

"If," replied Felicitas, calmly, "my children are faithful to Christ, they will attain eternal life with me; if from fear of death they should sacrifice to idols, they can expect nothing but death eternal."

The prefect was annoyed and distressed, but finding all his efforts fruitless, he reluctantly placed Felicitas in prison until the next day, when he called a public assembly in the great square before the Temple of Mars and again renewed his appeals to her.

"Take pity on your children, Felicitas!" he said. "They are now in the bloom of youth, and may yet possess the greatest honors and promotions."

"The pity which you desire me to feel," replied Felicitas proudly, "is really wickedness. Compliance to the compassion to which you exhort would make me the cruelest of mothers."

Then, turning to her seven sons, who stood by her side, she exclaimed, with a voice that rang clearly through the air and echoed against the buildings which surrounded the square, "My sons, look up to heaven, where your Christ with His saints expects you. By faith in His love, resist courageously unto death."

"We will," replied the young men all together in an enthusiastic tone, with a look of admiration and reverence at their mother, who seemed for a moment to be transfigured into a being not of earth.

"You are insolent indeed," exclaimed the prefect, greatly exasperated by the manner and speech of Felicitas and her sons, "thus in my presence to express contempt for the orders of our prince." And turning abruptly to his officers, he ordered the noble lady to be whipped.

But still desiring to preserve the young men, as soon as their mother had been removed for punishment, he called each of them to him in turn and used many arguments, mingled with threats, to induce them to sacrifice. But they all stood firm, and he ordered them all to be separately scourged and sent back to prison.

Felicitas never saw her noble sons again, but as she lay in the dreadful confinement of a dark, damp dungeon, there came to her from time to time the information that one or other of them had found rest in heaven by a violent death, after enduring many tortures. Januarius was smitten down with whips loaded with lead; Felix and Philip, the two next brothers, were beaten with sticks until they expired; Sylvanus, the fourth, was thrown over a deep precipice; and the three youngest, Alexander, Vitalis, and Martialis, were beheaded.

When the news of her last son's departure from the world reached the brave Felicitas, she folded her hands meekly and rejoiced that her influence and teaching had been so effectual. Four months later, she was called upon to lay her own head upon the block for Christ's sake, and she obeyed the command with such a sweet expression of countenance, and a resignation so remarkable, that her behavior at the last added greatly to the number of converts she had made in her lifetime.

Virtue Study

Recite Jeremiah 29:11, the memory verse for this week.

1. Why did Felicitas refuse to offer a sacrifice to the pagan gods?
2. Was she afraid to suffer for Christ?

What do these verses say about being courageous during persecution? What is the reason for trials? Why should we persevere?
- ♥ Romans 8:35–37
- ♥ Hebrews 10:32–36
- ♥ James 1:2–4
- ♥ 1 Peter 1:6–7

How did Felicitas live out 1 Peter 2:11–12?

WEEK 5 ~ DAY 1

An Indian Princess Guide, Part 1
By Edwin Legrand Sabin, 1918

This is the story of one young little Indian woman, who opened the trail across the continent. In March 1804, the United States took over the French province of Louisiana, which extended from the upper Mississippi River west to the Rocky Mountains.

These Western Indians were very different from the Eastern Indians. They rode horses and were accustomed to the rough buffalo chase and a wide range over vast treeless spaces.

To learn about the Indians and to find the Northwest Passage, the president sent Captain Meriwether Lewis and Captain William Clark on an expedition. In May 1804, they started up the Missouri River by boats from St. Louis.

The Corps of Discovery was an army expedition with twenty-three enlisted men, a hunter, a squad of boatmen, and Captain Clark's black slave, York. Their orders were to ascend the Missouri River to its head and, if possible, to cross the mountains and travel westward to the Columbia River and its mouth at the Pacific Ocean of the Oregon country. No white man knew what lay before them, for no white man had ever made the trip. The continent was large and mysterious. Would the men survive the wilds?

By the fall of 1804, they had gone safely as far as the towns of the Mandan Indians in central North Dakota. Here they wintered and met the little Bird Woman.

Her Indian name was Sacagawea, from two Minnetaree words meaning *bird* and *woman*. But she was not a Minnetaree, who were a division of the Sioux nation living in North Dakota near the Mandans. She was a Shoshone, or Snake, woman from the distant Rocky Mountains, who had been captured by the Minnetarees. These tribes, the Minnetarees of the plains and the Shoshones of the mountains, were always at war.

Still in her teens, she was now the wife of Toussaint Chaboneau, a leather-faced, leather-clad French-Canadian trader living with the Mandans. He had bought her from the Minnetarees—and how much he had paid in trade is not stated, but she was the daughter of a chief and was rated a good squaw. Toussaint had another wife, but he wanted a younger one. Therefore, he bought Sacagawea to mend his moccasins and greet him with a smile for his heart and warm water for his tired feet.

Chaboneau was engaged by Lewis and Clark as an interpreter. He and his wife moved to the camp of the white men. There, Sacagawea proved to be such a cheerful, willing little woman that

the captains and the men made much of her. And when, in February, a tiny boy arrived to her and Chaboneau, there was much delight. A baby in the camp helped to break the long dull spell of forty-below-zero weather.

It was a thousand miles to the Rocky or Shining Mountains if they followed the river trail. In the Mandan towns, and in the American camp, Sacagawea was the only person who had ever been as far as those mountains. They were the home of her people, but nearly three years had passed since she had been taken captive by the Minnetarees.

Many questions were asked of the young girl.

"Could she still speak the Shoshone tongue?"

"Certainly!" was Sacagawea's prompt answer.

"Did she remember the trail to the country of the Shoshones?"

"Yes!"

"Was there a way across the mountains?"

"Yes! Beyond some great falls in the Missouri there was a gate, by which the Shoshones came out of the mountains to hunt the buffalo on the plains. It was there that she had been captured by the Minnetarees."

"Would the Shoshone be friendly to the white men?"

"Yes, unless they were frightened by the white men."

"Would she like to go back to her own people?"

"Yes!"

In the spring they broke camp, and taking Chaboneau as interpreter in case the hostile Minnetarees were met, and little Sacagawea to find the land of the Shoshone, and tiny Pomp, the baby, as a peace sign to all tribes, with a picked party of thirty-one, the two captains started on up the swollen Missouri.

The Bird Woman proved a valuable asset. Of course she was used to roughing it, that was the life of an Indian woman—to do the hard work for the men, in camp and on the trail. But Sacagawea early showed good sense.

One day her husband Chaboneau almost capsized their canoe by his clumsiness. She neither shrieked nor jumped, but calmly reached out and gathered the floating articles. She saved stuff of much value, and the captains praised her. "She's a better man than her husband," asserted the admiring soldiers.

Virtue Study

Memory Verse: Romans 8:28. Write this verse on a 3 x 5 card and memorize it during the week.

1. How did Sacagawea end up in North Dakota?
2. How did she respond to her slavery?
3. What virtues did Sacagawea display?

Despite being a slave, Sacagawea was not bitter. What do these verses say about bitterness and not holding a grudge?
- ♥ Leviticus 19:18
- ♥ Ephesians 4:31–32
- ♥ Hebrews 12:14–15

What advice does Ephesians 6:5–8 have about how slaves should behave? Did Sacagawea do this?

As Christians, we willingly become slaves to Christ. Read Romans 6:16–22. What does it means to be a slave of righteousness?

WEEK 5 ~ DAY 2

An Indian Princess Guide, Part 2
By Edwin Legrand Sabin, 1918

After hard travel, fighting the swift current, the strong winds, storms of rain and sleet, and monster grizzly bears, the expedition arrived at the Great Falls as the Bird Woman had promised.

She had ridden and waded and trudged like the rest. She had carried her baby on her back, and she had built the fires for her husband, and cooked his meals, and kept up with the men, and had not complained nor lagged.

At the Great Falls, she was not so certain of the best route. This was a strange country to her, although she had known that the falls were here. The Shining Mountains were in sight, and the land of the Shoshones lay yonder, to the southwest.

The captains chose what seemed to be the best route by water and headed on to the southwest. Sacagawea gazed anxiously, right, left, and before. Her heart was troubled. She hoped to find her people for herself, but she also desired to help the great captains. The fate of the whole party depended upon her—and she was just a young woman!

The Shoshone did not come down by this way. It was too far north; it was the land of their enemies the Blackfeet and the Minnetarees, of whom they were deathly afraid. They were a timid mountain folk, poorly armed to fight the Sioux, who had obtained guns from traders down the Missouri. After a time the river narrowed still more, and between rough banks it poured out from a canyon of high cliffs.

"The Gate of the Mountains, isn't it?" passed the hopeful word. Sacagawea agreed. She had heard of this very "gate," where the river burst into the first plains.

"When we come to the place where the river splits into three parts, that is Shoshone country—my people will be there."

On forged the boats, poled and hauled and rowed, while the men's soggy moccasins rotted into pieces and the mosquitoes bit fiercely. The two captains explored by land. Hunting was forbidden, lest the reports of the guns alarm the Shoshones. Abandoned Indian campsites were found, but no sight of the Shoshones.

Captain Clark, the "Red Head" as he was called, took the advance, by land, to look for the Indians. Captain Lewis, the young "Long Knife Chief," commanded the boats. Small United States flags were erected in the bows of each as a peace signal. The boats reached an open place, where the river did indeed split into several branches.

"The Three Forks," nodded Sacagawea brightly. "These are the Three Forks. We are on the right trail to the land of my people. Now I know."

The party proceeded at top speed. The southwest fork seemed to be the best for boating. At the next camp, Sacagawea was more excited.

"She says here is the spot where the Shoshone camp was surprised by the Minnetaree and chased into the timber," announced Drouillard the hunter. "The Minnetaree killed four warriors. She was captured here herself."

Hurrah! The trail was getting warm. The canoes had to be hauled by towlines, with Sacagawea proudly riding in one of them and helping to push with a pole. She had not been here since she was a girl of eleven or twelve, but she recognized more landmarks.

"That is what the Shoshone call the Beaver's Head," proclaimed Chaboneau. "The Shoshone spend their summers across the mountains. She thinks we are sure to meet some on this side who are hunting buffalo."

Captain Lewis took three men and struck out to find an Indian trail and follow it into the mountains.

"I'll not come back until I've met with the Shoshones," he asserted.

Virtue Study

Work on Romans 8:28, the memory verse for this week.

1. Pretend you are Sacagawea and try to imagine what she was feeling as she neared her home. Share about your thoughts.
2. Why were the Americans depending on her to find her people?

Sacagawea had learned to be content in her new life, but she still longed to go home. The Bible has a lot to say about this not being our home. Look up these verses and think about the eternal home that God has prepared for those who live for Him.
- ♥ 2 Corinthians 5:1–10
- ♥ Philippians 3:20–21
- ♥ Hebrews 11:10 and 13

WEEK 5 ~ DAY 3

An Indian Princess Guide, Part 3
By Edwin Legrand Sabin, 1918

He was gone a long time. The shallow river, full of rapids and shoals, curved and forked and steadily shrank. But although Sacagawea eagerly gazed and murmured to herself, no Indians appeared.

The water was icy cold because of the snow that lingered in the mountains of Montana even during the month of August. The nights were cold too. Game grew scarce. Three thousand miles had been logged off from St. Louis. But unless the company could get guides and horses from the Shoshones and travel rapidly, they would be caught by winter storms and likely enough starve or be forced to go back without accomplishing their goal.

By August 16, Captain Lewis had not returned. Captain Clark set out on foot, with Sacagawea and Chaboneau, to walk across country. The Shoshones simply must be found. The toiling boats rounded a great bend, and a shout arose.

"There's Clark! He's sighted Indians, hasn't he?"

"So has Sacagawea! Sure she has! See?"

"Indians on horseback, boys! Hooray!"

For Captain Clark, yonder up the curve, was holding high his hand, palm front, in the peace sign. Sacagawea had run ahead, little Pomp bobbing in the pack on her back, and she danced as she ran.

"That means she sees her own people!" panted Cruzatte the chief boatman, who was a trapper and trader, too, and knew Indians. "There they come, on the horses. Hooray!"

What a relief! The Indians were prancing and singing. They made the captain mount one of the horses, and all hustled on for an Indian camp.

By the time the hurrying canoes arrived, Sacagawea and another woman had rushed into each other's arms. Presently they and the captain and Chaboneau had entered a large lodge built of willow branches. The Captain Lewis squad was here too. The men had come down out of the mountains, by a pass, with the Shoshones. The Shoshones had been afraid of them—the first white men ever seen by the band. Old Drouillard, the hunter, had argued with them in sign language and with a few Shoshone words that he knew.

It had looked like war—it had looked like peace—and it had looked like war, and death, again. Finally, before he could persuade them, the captain had delivered over his guns and had promised them to be their prisoner if they did not find, down below, one of their own women acting as the white men's guide.

But now all was well. The sight of Sacagawea saved the day. The other woman, whom she hugged, had been captured by the Minnetarees at the same time as Sacagawea and had escaped.

Best of all was the fact that the chief of the band was Sacagawea's brother. He had mourned her as dead, but now he and she wept together. Truly, he had reason to be grateful to these white strangers who had treated her so well.

Much relieved by finding the Indians, the captains bought horses and hired guides. The Shoshones were very friendly.

There was little delay. The mountains should be crossed at once, before winter closed the trails. To the surprise and delight of all the company, Sacagawea announced that she was going with them to see the Great Salt Water. Somehow, she preferred the white men to her own people. She had been weeping constantly. Most of her relatives and old friends had died or been killed during her absence. Her new friends she loved. They were a wonderful set, these white men—and the Red Head, Captain Clark, was the finest of all.

Six horses had been bought. Five were packed with the supplies, Sacagawea and little Pomp were mounted upon the sixth, and the whole company, escorted by the Shoshones, marched over the pass to Chief Cameahwait's principal camp.

From there, with twenty-seven horses and one mule, with the happy Bird Woman and the beady-eyed Pomp, the two captains and their men took the trail for the Great Salt Water, one thousand miles toward the setting sun. Ah, but a tough trail that proved: across the Bitter Root Mountains, all up and down, with scarcely a level spot to sleep on; with the snow to the horses' bellies and the men's thighs; with the game failing, until even a horse's head was treasured. And the Bird Woman, riding with the exhausted men, never complained, but kept her eyes fixed to the low country and the big river and dreams of the Great Salt Water.

Once, in the midst of starvation, she brought out a small piece of bread that she had carried all the way from the Mandan town. She gave it to Captain Clark that he might eat it. A brave and faithful heart had Sacagawea.

Struggling down out of the mountains, at the end of September, they changed to canoes. The Pierced Noses, or Nez Percé Indians, were friendly, and now, on to the Columbia and thence on to the sea, Sacagawea's presence showed that they came in peace. For when the tribes saw the strange white warriors, they said, "This cannot be a war party. They have a squaw and a papoose. We will meet with them."

Virtue Study

Work on Romans 8:28, the memory verse for this week.

1. Who did Sacagawea meet at the Indian camp?
2. Why did Sacagawea decide to go with the explorers?
3. How did she protect the group from hostile tribes?

Does her story remind you of anyone in the Bible? Read Genesis 37 and 39–50 and answer these questions:
- ♥ Why did Joseph's brothers sell him?
- ♥ How did Joseph respond to his slavery?
- ♥ How did he become the most powerful person in Egypt?
- ♥ What explanation did Joseph give in Genesis 50:20 for why the events happened the way they did?

WEEK 5 ~ DAY 4

An Indian Princess Guide, Part 4
By Edwin Legrand Sabin, 1918

That winter was spent a few miles from the Pacific, near the mouth of the Columbia River in the present-day state of Washington.

Only once did the Bird Woman complain. The ocean was out of sight from the camp. Chaboneau, her husband, seemed to think that she was made for only work, cooking, mending, and tending the baby.

"You stay by the lodge fire. That is the place for women," he rebuked. Whereupon Sacagawea took the bit in her teeth (a very unusual thing for a squaw to do) and went straight to Captain Clark, her friend.

"What is the matter, Sacagawea?"

"I come a long way, Captain. I carry my baby; I've suffered cold, hunger, sickness. I showed you the trail. I say 'Shoshone peoples here,' and you find Shoshones. You get horses, food, and a guide. When Indians see me and my Pomp, they say 'This is no war party,' and they are kind to you. When you get hungry for bread, I give you one little piece that I carry all the way from Mandan. I try to be a good woman. I work hard, same as the men.

Now I've been here all this time, near the salt water that I traveled many days to see—and I haven't seen it yet. There is a big fish too. Others go to see the water, but I stay. Nobody ask me. My man, he say, 'You tend baby!' I—I feel bad, Captain." And she hid her face in her blanket.

"You shall, Sacagawea, and see the salt water and the big fish," declared Captain Clark. "Chaboneau can stay home and tend the baby!"

However, the Bird Woman took little Pomp, and they viewed in wonderment the rolling, surging, thundering ocean, and the immense whale, one hundred and five feet long, that had been cast ashore. It is safe to assert that to the end of her days, Sacagawea never forgot these awesome sights.

In the spring of 1806, the homeward journey was begun. On the Missouri side of the mountains the Bird Woman was detailed to help Captain Clark find a separate trail, to the Yellowstone River.

And this she did, in splendid fashion, for when the party knew not which way was the best way out of the surrounding hills to the plains, she picked the landmarks, and though she had not been here in many years, she showed the gap that led over and down and brought them straight to the sunken canoes.

On August 14, the whole company was at the Mandan towns once more. After her absence of a year and a half, and her journey of six thousand miles, bearing little Pomp (another great traveler)

Sacagawea hustled ashore to entertain the other women with her vivid stories.

The captains offered to take Chaboneau and Sacagawea and Pomp on down to St. Louis. The Bird Woman would gladly have gone. She wanted to learn more of the white people's ways.

But Chaboneau respectfully declined. He said that it would be a strange country and that he could not make a living there; later, he might send his boy to be educated by the captains. That was all.

So he was paid wages amounting to five hundred dollars and thirty-three cents for the service he gave. What happened to her after this is not certain. Some sources say she died in 1812 and others that she lived till 1884. Although she did not receive a monetary reward for her services, the rich legacy that she left has not been forgotten by the American people. A mountain peak in Montana has been named Sacagawea Peak. A bronze statue of her has been erected in the city park of Portland, Oregon. Another statue has been erected in the state capitol at Bismarck, North Dakota. The people of the great United States remember the loving services of the brave little Bird Woman who courageously helped make the expedition across the continent a success.

Virtue Study

Work on Romans 8:28, the memory verse for this week.

1. How did Sacagawea's journey end?
2. How do you think she felt after the trip was over?
3. What virtues did Sacagawea have?

Look up some of those virtues in a concordance and read what the Bible says about those character traits.

So many times we do things to draw attention to ourselves. Sacagawea would probably be surprised that she is remembered two hundred years later. We too need to do our work without expecting big rewards here on earth. Read Matthew 6:1–4. What are some ways that you can do things for God instead of man?

Sacagawea was eager to help Lewis and Clark. In the Bible we read a story about a Shunammite woman who was eager to help Elisha. Both of these women asked nothing in return for their service. Read 2 Kings 4:8–37, and answer these questions:
- ♥ What did the Shunammite woman do for Elisha?
- ♥ How did he respond?

Box of Visual Reminders

Sacagawea loved blue beads. During their travels, the Corps used beads to trade with the Indians for food and other supplies. Blue beads were highly valued. Put a blue bead in your box to remind yourself of Sacagawea's eagerness to serve, her forgiving heart, and her courage.

WEEK 5 ~ DAY 5

A Providential Escape
By Mr. Blaisdell and Mr. Ball, 1911

During the late 1700s, Missouri was a wilderness, and only a few brave pioneers lived there because the Indians were very fierce. The famous frontiersman Daniel Boone lived near the Missouri River in the district of St. Charles. A neighbor to the Boones was a family named Patterson, who had also moved from Kentucky.

The Pattersons had a daughter named Helen, who was about eighteen years of age. One day in June of 1809, all the Patterson family except Helen were away from home. The girl stood by the open door, busily cooking. All of a sudden, the lonely cabin was surrounded by a band of Indians. Helen knew well enough that it would be useless to cry for help or try to escape. One of the warriors, who could talk a little English, told her that if she made an outcry they would kill her.

The Indians ransacked the cabin and made ready to take away such things as they could easily carry. In a few minutes the whole band, with Helen as their captive, set off afoot to the north through the forest.

"Oh!" cried the girl, "what will Father and Mother think when they come back and find that I have been carried away?"

She had with her a ball of white yarn. As they went through the forest, she occasionally broke off bits of yarn and dropped them along the way. She knew that her father and friends would follow in pursuit and that the yarn would serve as a guide. An Indian caught the girl at it and raised his tomahawk as if to kill her. The ball of yarn was taken from her, and she was closely watched for fear she would try again to mark the trail.

During the afternoon, the Indians became uneasy. It was plain to Helen that her friends were in pursuit and that the warriors knew it. About sunset, two of the Indians went back to find out the real state of affairs. The rest of the band had a long and exciting talk until their comrades returned.

It was now dark. The night was cloudy, and the rumbling of distant thunder gave warning of a storm. The Indians crossed the creek they had been following and led the girl into the deep woods about a mile from the ford. They then tied her wrists together, pulled her arms above her head, and fastened them with strips of deerskin to the branch of a tree.

"Indians now go ford, and hide, and kill white man," muttered the Indian, who could speak a little broken English.

Helen was now alone in the woods, and tied so tight that she could not hope to escape. Her fingers and wrists began to swell, and she was almost wild with pain and fear. She tried with all her strength to get free, but it was of no use. She knew that the Indians might come back at any moment and kill her, and she prayed to God to send somebody to set her free.

Then suddenly a storm moved into the area. Lightning lit up the dark woods, and the peals of thunder came louder and louder. Down came the rain in torrents and drenched the captive girl. Once more she tried to escape, and this time her hands slipped easily through the rain-soaked thongs of deerskin. It took but a moment to untie her feet. Then, fleet as a deer, she ran toward the ford.

"If I can only get there in time to warn my father and brothers!"

At last, tired out, she sat under a tree in the pouring rain and eagerly strained her eyes to catch a glimpse of her rescuers. In a short time, she caught sight of some persons moving through the forest.

Who could it be? Might it be some of the Indians coming back for her? Could it indeed be her father and brothers?

"Father! Father!" she cried in a low voice.

"Helen, dear girl, is that you?" came the reply.

In another moment she was held in the arms of her father and her two brothers. While the two sturdy sons of Daniel Boone were praising her for her courage.

They now made their way home in safety over a new trail. Helen's mother, nearly frantic at the loss of her daughter, was overcome with joy at her return.

Virtue Study

Recite Romans 8:28, the memory verse for this week.

1. What virtues did Helen have?
2. How did she respond in an emergency? What can we learn from her example of staying calm?
3. What did Helen do when she needed help?
4. Do you think she believed God would answer her prayer? Why or why not?

What do these verses say about prayer?
- ♥ Romans 8:26
- ♥ Ephesians 6:18

What does this verse say about being calm?
- ♥ Isaiah 7:4

In Matthew 8 there is the story of Jesus reacting calmly in the middle of a storm. Read Matthew 8:23–27 and answer these questions:
- ♥ How did Jesus react to the storm?
- ♥ How can we as followers of Christ face the storms of life?
- ♥ What kind of power does Jesus have that allowed Him to calm storms?

WEEK 6 ~ DAY 1

A Kind Woman Who Helped Luther
By Charles Carleton Coffin, 1879

Martin Luther's father was a poor miner, and his mother was a stern woman. His teacher was also severe, and the poor boy received many beatings. Because Martin showed promise in Latin, his parents sent him to a school taught by monks. To provide food for himself, he had to go through town and sing for his bread. Each morning he would hope to find a generous person to give him some food.

On a cold morning, a band of students passed through the streets of Eisenach, singing from door to door, hoping thus to procure their daily bread. Turned away from many houses, oftentimes rudely, tired in body, hungry, and sick at heart, at last the weary band stopped before the house of Conrad Cotta, the rich burgher. Never had they left this door hungry. Here they always met kind looks, cheering words, and generous assistance. Today they looked for a similar reception, and they began their carol. So sweetly did their fresh young voices ring out the beautiful hymns that one would not have imagined they came from aching hearts.

Anxiously they awaited some sign from within. Their prayer was answered, for the door opened and a good woman appeared.

She seemed like a saint with a human smile. Her hands were outstretched with kindness and her smile seemed to speak to the human heart and cheer it. The expectant children received their customary greeting and assistance.

As Ursula was about to reenter the house, she caught sight of Martin Luther, looking so pale and feeble that all her motherly pity was aroused. "Poor Martin," she said, and taking him by the hand, she led him into the house.

The kind act came not one moment too soon, for the boy had scarcely crossed the threshold before he fell fainting at her feet. As she hovered over him, ministering to him with tenderness, anxiety, and gentleness, a new resolution took root in her pitying heart: a resolution that would give the little street singer a home of love and comfort, and which would affect his character and later life.

When Martin recovered, he was in a warm, cheerful, homelike room. He was greeted by the kind voice of a matronly little woman with silvery hair, brown eyes full of compassion, and rosy cheeks that were dimpled with the sweetest of smiles.

In her hearty, cheery way, she bid him cast away his cares, his anxieties, and all those things that disturbed him, and begin a happier life in her home. Thus, Martin Luther was received into the Cotta family, where he remained four years. A new life dawned on him. Up to that point, his childhood had been one of suffering, poverty, and hardship. He had passed through darkness and was coming to the light. His graver, sterner nature had been developed, and it was now time for the brighter part.

Luther's childhood, although it developed in his nature lasting qualities of great worth, gave him also some which, unless taken away, would have been very injurious and unhappy. These were but temporary, and under the care of the watchful Ursula Cotta, they disappeared. She knew the longings and pains of his young heart. She offered him sympathy and love, soothed its aching, and satisfied its yearning. He met no repulses, no rebukes, but ready answers to all his inquiries and eager questionings.

Luther's early training had imparted to him a shrinking timidity. He was silent, gloomy, and moody. Ursula Cotta, with her warm, bright cheerfulness, her sunshiny happiness, changed his dark world. She dissipated the gloom and called to light all the hidden brightness of his nature, and he was no longer silent and solitary, but the leader in the children's games, their songs, and their conversations. The change was wrought by the quick insight, marvelous tact, and careful attention of Frau Cotta.

She had long, earnest talks with him, inviting his confidence, appreciating it, and interesting herself in all his thoughts. She found out his love for music and cultivated it. She gave him a flute, and she would accompany him in song. Thus many happy hours were spent together. He would confide to her his hopes, his sorrows, and his plans, and looking into her earnest, loving eyes, he would always find sympathy.

What a truly blessed life was that within the burgher Cotta's house! Here there was ever an atmosphere of love, where nothing could exist but happiness. Ursula was the good angel who imparted this wondrous charm to the household: a true woman, with delicate insight, sympathies, tenderness, compassion, and all those womanly traits that ensure happiness to those around. Martin knew and acknowledged how much he owed to this kind Christian woman's influence. Of her he has said, "There is nothing sweeter on earth than the heart of a woman in which pity dwells."

Virtue Study

Memory Verse: Proverbs 31:26. Write this verse on a 3 x 5 card and memorize it during the week.

1. Why was Luther hungry?
2. What did Ursula do?
3. How did her act of kindness change the course of history?

What do these verses say about helping the poor?
- ♥ Proverbs 31:20
- ♥ Isaiah 58:6–11
- ♥ Ezekiel 16:49
- ♥ Matthew 25:35–45

What do these verses say about compassion?
- ♥ Psalm 103:1–4
- ♥ Colossians 3:12
- ♥ 1 Peter 3:8

WEEK 6 ~ DAY 2

Running to the Truth
By Emma Louise Parry, 1882

In the 1500s, it was common for noble families in financial problems to send their unwanted daughters to a convent. It was a "family arrangement" practiced generation after generation in noble German households. In 1509, a young girl of the family of von Bora was put in a convent. Here, Katherine found her aunt, Magdalena von Bora, who been the victim in the previous generation of this unjust custom.

In the first quarter of the sixteenth century, however, a change came over the hitherto quiet and peaceful convent near Grimma, in Nimpstchen, where Katherine von Bora was housed. In 1523, there were among the sisterhood several young women with active minds ever ready to discern truth and true hearts willing to follow it. They were enthusiasts, with minds open and fresh to receive new ideas. They had been sent here by their parents at an early age before they had reason enough to choose for themselves. Yet they entered into the true spirit of the Order. Day by day, they attended service in the morning and evening, said their prayers using the beads that reminded them of how many times they should say certain things, chanted during Mass, and did penance by suffering labor or pain for their sins.

Often severe punishment, self-inflicted, would follow a girl who had wandering thoughts, for their restless minds would, despite restraint, wander to the world beyond the gray convent walls. Quiet, peaceful, happy hours too they had, over their embroidery and sewing, while one of their number read aloud. Works of charity filled in their time, and many were the blessings that arose from the sick and the destitute as the holy sisters walked among them. Among the books that came from Eisenach, from Cotta's printing press, were several translations of Dr. Luther's.

The attention of the young nuns was aroused. They read and reread them. They were wonder-stricken but doubtful. Finally, they were overflowing with enthusiasm for the Doctor of Wittenberg, and convinced of his truth. What he wrote must be true—their reason and judgment confirmed his words, and surely these passages from the New Testament came from God.

Oh, then, how far astray from his teaching had been their lives! What good had been done by their penance, scourges, and punishments? They read that there is freedom in forgiveness of sins, salvation is free to all, works are dead, it is faith that justifies. Self can do nothing, it is God through Christ who saves. All this was new to them.

Next came Luther's treatise upon monasteries. This was another revelation to them. They had lived with the conviction that a life within the sacred walls of the convent was most pleasing, most holy in the sight of God—for had they not wedded the church and cast all else aside? But Dr. Luther said that life in a convent is not the true Christian life, that their lives were no purer, no better, no holier than those of ordinary mortals, that the life of a true follower is not one of seclusion, but to stand in the midst of the world and yet apart from it. The nuns of Nimpstch were awakened to new ideas of life.

They caught the truth, they felt it, and they determined to act upon it. The serenity of the convent was broken up, for the young nuns speedily made known their beliefs, and they told the truth to their older sisters. The elder ones were unconvinced: they looked with sorrow, even with hatred, upon the young heretics, whom they ridiculed with the name "the Lutheran sisters." More books were received at Nimpstch, and deeper and warmer became their enthusiasm for Dr. Luther and his words. Their bonds irritated them, their duties were unendurable, and their ever-present thought was to break their chains and get beyond their prison walls. Faith, and a life conformed to that faith, was the idea which possessed them.

Finally, they resolved to use some means of escape, as all their letters to friends and relatives brought them no hope of release. They wrote to Dr. Luther, informing him of their troubles and their desire to escape and asking aid. Tradition says that nine of the nuns, all who dared the venture, met in the cell of Katherine von Bora, who planned the rescue.

A letter to Dr. Luther brought about the desired result. A night was appointed, and within the convent the young nuns were preparing to leave their narrow world and enter into the trials of an unknown greater one.

Night came, and the nine women waited before the high stone walls. Two brave men, Master Leonard Koppe of Torgau and Wolfgang Tomitzsch, were ready to assist them. The nuns managed to climb over the high wall, and soon they stood upon the ground, outside the convent, free from its forms and duties—free to worship as their hearts directed.

They entered a covered wagon that the two men had brought with them for the purpose. It was filled with herring barrels, wherein the women might hide if necessary. As the wagon wheels began to roll, the former nuns realized that they were escaping from bondage, but more than that, they were running to the truth.

Finally the wagon reached an old Augustinian convent. Here the women rejoiced to behold, face-to-face, their beloved Doctor Luther.

Several persons kindly received them into their houses, and soon all of them were settled in Wittenberg: these nine nuns, who with courage and a brave independence shook off the unnatural bonds of the Roman church and joyfully encountered any trial that would open the way to a true life in Christ—having found the truth which makes men free.

Virtue Study

Work on Proverbs 31:26, the memory verse for this week.

1. What virtues did Katherine have?
2. Why was Katherine placed in a convent?
3. How did Katherine and the other nuns come to know the truth of Scripture?

In the convent, Katherine was trying to earn her way into heaven. What does the Bible say about that? Read James 2:14–26 and share your thoughts about them.

These nuns eagerly embraced the truth of Scripture. Read Acts 17:11. What does God's Word say about how to determine if a new teaching is true or false?

WEEK 6 ~ DAY 3

The Wife of Martin Luther, Part 1
By Emma Louise Parry, 1882

Among the nuns who escaped from Nimpstch was Katherine von Bora. She was born in Saxony in 1499 and belonged to one of the noble families of the land. At the age of ten, she was sent to the convent, where she remained in comparative happiness for several years. Once she was awakened to the truth of Scripture, she escaped from the convent with eight others and found friends in Luther's city. A burgomaster in Wittenberg kindly opened his home to her. Luther thought the best thing for the former nuns would be for them to marry.

Luther found more trouble in his matrimonial schemes for the grave and dignified Katherine than he'd had with the other nuns. She was the noblest of them all. Although not beautiful, yet there was majesty in her manner; earnestness and expression in her dark eyes; character in the large but firm mouth; and intellect in the high, smooth forehead. Until one was more acquainted with her, she seemed cold and reserved—so much so that the great Doctor himself was awed—but after having won her friendship, there was seen a warmth of heart, a friendliness, and a kind, open, winning manner that was particularly engaging.

Jeremy Baumgartner was the first to try to win the love of this daughter of the house of Bora. But such honor was not for him, nor for Dr. Glatz, whom Luther highly recommended. Katherine was not quite as frank as Priscilla, the Pilgrim maiden, for she did not say directly, "Why don't you speak for yourself, Martin." But she communicated the fact that the Doctor himself was her favorite to his friend Amsdorf, who was not long in producing order out of the confusion.

On June 13, 1525, Luther, accompanied by three of his friends, entered the house of Amsdorf, and with little ceremony, but great briefness and abruptness, he asked the astonished Katherine to become his wife. They were immediately betrothed, and before the day had closed, Luther and Katherine, monk and nun, were married. He took his bride, the dignified, graceful Katherine, to the old Augustinian convent to make a home for him, for deep within his heart there was the true German love and longing for a home and fireside to which he could claim exclusive right.

A new life began in the old monastery, and the dark gloom and silence of the convent were dispelled and banished by the cheerfulness and brightness which Katherine brought.

The life of Martin and Ketha (as he loved to call her), approached very near to the ideal married life. When Martin Luther married, there was not the deep, warm, earnest love for Katherine that she gave him. He said at the time, "I am not on fire with love," but it came, and as the years passed, it became deeper, warmer, more earnest—the full, strong love such as a heart like that of Martin Luther, with his great strong nature, is alone capable of holding.

Katherine had a firm, strong character. She was capable of supporting and helping in trials, not sinking beneath them and proving a burden. She had a quick, understanding mind, and she could readily appreciate the thoughts of the great Doctor, although she was not able to pursue them to the depth of their meaning. She was warmly interested in all his work, and by her interest and enthusiasm she increased that of Luther.

She helped him as far as she was able in his intellectual pursuits, by reading to him and writing for him. She relieved him of many duties in order that his precious time might be devoted to the cause for which he was born. She carried on all his correspondence, when capable, and those letters that she could not arrange herself, she kept him from forgetting. No household affairs were allowed to trouble him, for Ketha had great managing abilities. All the financial affairs of the house were well managed, and without a thought by the master of it. The farm at Zolsdorf, which Martin had given to his wife, was kept in excellent condition; buildings were erected and the land was tilled.

Not only were the outward affairs kept in this flourishing condition, not only was Madam Luther a financier and manager, but within the house there was a home. Here she was the tender, loving wife; the wise and good mother. Here all the gentler womanly qualities of her nature shone forth—to comfort, soothe, and sympathize. She loved to make the home cheerful and happy, to aid her husband by making his surroundings bright, so that no anxieties should disturb his work, but that when his aching, weary brain sought relief, it could be found at the peaceful fireside.

Virtue Study

Work on Proverbs 31:26, the memory verse for this week.

1. How did Martin and Katherine get married?
2. What benefits did Luther gain by having a good wife?
3. What virtues did Katherine have?

What do these verses say about how a woman should live?
- ♥ Proverbs 11:16
- ♥ Proverbs 12:4
- ♥ Proverbs 14:1
- ♥ Titus 2:3–5

Read Acts 16:11–15. What did the woman in Acts do after she became a Christian?

WEEK 6 ~ DAY 4

The Wife of Martin Luther, Part 2
By Emma Louise Parry, 1882

Katherine showed tact in adapting herself to the mood of her husband so that she was always companionable to him. When he was heartsick with the severe trials and bitter criticisms that were poured upon him, it was her comfort that soothed him.

When fatigued and downcast, she would sit at his side, sewing or embroidering, and speak healing words to him—verses from the Scriptures that were a balm to his ruffled spirit. She would turn his thoughts from the grave and serious by asking him questions—often amusing—with the greatest simplicity. She was a good listener and would pay attention interestedly to any subject that he preferred talking upon. Together they worked in love for the sick and the poor.

Oftentimes the monastery would resemble a hospital, for the sick and the poor ever met kindness from its inmates. Friends came to visit them, and after being led through the garden by Dr. Luther (who displayed with pride Ketha's vegetables and flowers), and having enjoyed supper under the trees, the company would have music before they left the Wittenberg convent. Everyone praised the domestic happiness and acknowledged that it had been well for Martin Luther to marry.

Luther's life, filled with cares, anxieties, and dangers, needed sympathy and outside enjoyment to sustain and refresh it. It would have been hard for the Reformer had he no bright hours to make him forget his troubles and strengthen him for greater trials, nor would his work have been so effective. That well of tenderness and love in his nature which his domestic life reveals would never have been known. And so this marriage, which the whole Catholic world cried out against and pronounced cursed, proved blessed, and brought much good to the Reformation, and so to the Christian world.

The peaceful life at the monastery was often disturbed. Martin Luther would be obliged to go forth into the world, meet his opponents, and cope with them. Many letters were exchanged. From these letters we see another phase of Martin's many-sided character. Here he displayed a good-humored, playful, fun-loving spirit, which had before been entirely hidden under his soberness.

He was strongly attached to his wife, home, and children. Kindly he writes to his beloved Ketha, laughing at her fears for his safety, playfully chiding her for her loneliness, and signing himself "thy old lover." That Katherine von Bora still retained her dignity is apparent, for in these letters she is addressed as "Mea domina Ketha," "Doctress Luther," "My lord Kate," "Sir Kate," etc. Not only letters, but packages, medicines, and pictures did the careful wife send to him to show her concern and love. But the forebodings of Katherine were realized at last, and Martin Luther returned no more to his beloved Wittenberg home.

Did no clouds invade their happy household? Naturally there were, since they were human. But whatever were the shadows, they are unknown, entirely obscured by the sunshine of their everyday life. Many of the Wittenbergers found fault with the Doctor's wife on account of her haughty spirit. Some accused her of being proud. Yet, how could she well avoid it? Was not her husband Martin Luther? Was it not a commendable thing in her to take pride in that fact? Luther himself has given us the highest praise for Katherine von Bora. Thinking of her and his happy home, he writes, "The greatest gift of God is a pious, amiable spouse, who fears God, loves her home, and with whom one can live in perfect peace and confidence." After his death, in his will were found words of approval that must have been precious to her sorrowing heart: "My Ketha has always been a gentle, pious, and faithful wife to me."

After the death of her husband, she lived through seven years of poverty, persecution, and loneliness before she broke the bonds of earth. Yet through it all she still maintained that womanly dignity and heroism which belonged to her.

It is a sad thing to know that the world quickly forgot its debt to the great Reformer, and that no response met the pathetic appeals for help that came again and again from the widow of Martin Luther. Sad it is that she who had cheered one who brought cheer to the world found none to cheer her in those years of poverty, flight, and uninterrupted calamity! It is not alone because of the fact that Katherine von Bora was the wife of the leader of the Reformation that she is given historic notice. Independent of this, powerful as it is, she has earned a high place among the world's heroines by her own individual, strong character—her own bold, eventful, and influential life.

Virtue Study

Work on Proverbs 31:26, the memory verse for this week.

In Genesis 2:15–25, God explains why He made woman. How did Katherine fit this need in Martin's life?

Katherine was truly a "helpmeet" to her husband. Look up the word "helpmeet" and write down the definition.

How was she able to help her husband with his important work?

Think about the great cloud of witnesses that Hebrews 12:1 talks about. What kind of advice do you think Katherine would have for young ladies today?

Box of Visual Reminders

Look in a hymnal for songs by Martin Luther. When you find one that has encouraged you, write the words on a piece of paper and put it in your box. (You could also print the words off the Internet instead of writing them.) When you see it, remember how Katherine helped him in his important work. One of Luther's most famous hymns is "A Mighty Fortress is Our God."

WEEK 6 ~ DAY 5

Luther's Little Girl
By Cortlandt Van Rensselaer, 1856

On May 4, 1529, Katherine von Bora gave birth to a healthy daughter. This daughter was named Magdalena after Katherine's maiden aunt, who lived with them. Aunt Magdalena had been a nun, but she followed her niece's example and left the convent to become a Protestant.

Magdalena Luther was a child of singular depth of character: amiable, affectionate, and deeply religious. "Without the ordinary failings of children," her father testified that she had never done an act requiring parental reproof.

In her thirteenth year, Magdalena was taken by her heavenly Father from her earthly parents. Courageously and steadily she passed through death, and Luther, at the bedside of his dying child, was the same hero that had appeared before the Electors and the Diet.

During her illness he said, "I love her very much, but Father, if it be Thy will to take her hence, I bow entirely to Thee."

Standing by her bed, he said, "Magdalena, you are happy to stay with your father here, and willing to go to your Father there."

She replied, "Yes, dear Father, as God wills it."

"Dear child! The spirit is willing, but the flesh is weak," and turning around, he added, "I love her very dearly. If the flesh is so strong, what will the spirit be?"

A profound impression was made upon all of Luther's acquaintances as they saw a man of such rugged strength overcome with emotion by the side of his dying child.

As she became weaker and was failing, he fell upon his knees at her bedside and wept bitterly, and prayed God to deliver her. Soon after, she breathed her last in her father's arms. On the day of the funeral, Luther could not tear himself away from the coffin in which the child's body had been placed.

He stood by it and said, as he looked at her, "Dear Lena, you will rise again, and shine like a star, yes, a sun. Now that she has gone, I am happy in spirit, but in the flesh, I am very sad. The flesh will not be put down, and parting grieves one very much. It is strange that, while I know that she is certainly at peace, and that all is well with her, I should yet be so sorry."

When his friends told him that they were grieved for his loss, he replied, "You should rejoice that I have sent a saint to heaven."

While they were throwing the earth upon the coffin, he said, "There is a resurrection of the body." On his way to the house, he spoke, very earnestly, to his friends: "If my Magdalena could return to life, and bring me the wealth of the Ottoman Empire, I would not have her. Oh! It is well for her! Blessed are the dead who die in the Lord. Who dies so has certainly everlasting life, and I would that I, and my children, and all of you, might go, for evil times are coming."

Katherine was plunged by this event into the deepest grief, and Luther comforted her most affectionately. "Dear Kate, remember that where she has gone, she is very well, but flesh and blood do as flesh and blood; it is the spirit that is full of praise and is willing. Children do not argue, but believe as they are told. All is simple with them: they die without pain or anguish, and without contention with death or bodily distress, just as they fall asleep."

Virtue Study

Recite Proverbs 31:26, the memory verse for this week.

1. Who was Magdalena?
2. What influence did her life have on those around her?
3. What virtues did she have?

Death is a sad part of life. It's always hard for those left behind to live without their loved ones. In Genesis, we learn about how Adam and Eve's sin brought death into the world. Read these verses and think about how death entered the world through sin.
- ♥ Genesis 2:16–17
- ♥ Genesis 3:14–19

In Romans, we learn that Jesus conquered death. Read these verses and talk about how Adam brought death and Jesus brought life.
- ♥ Romans 5:12
- ♥ Romans 5:18–19

What do these verses say about life and death?
- ♥ Psalm 116:15
- ♥ 1 Corinthians 15:22–26
- ♥ Hebrews 2:14–15

Box of Visual Reminders

Magdalena brought joy to her parents. After she died, their comfort was in knowing that she was with her heavenly Father. Place a cross in your box (you could make one out of Popsicle sticks), and when you see it, remember how Christ conquered death.

WEEK 7 ~ DAY 1

Keeper of the Light
By Gustav Kobbe, 1897

The Matinicus Rock light station stood upon a huge granite rock off the southeastern entrance to Penobscot Bay, Maine, about twenty-two miles out to sea. Abbie Burgess's father was keeper of the rock from 1853 to 1861. In January 1856, when she was a teenager, he left her in charge of the lights while he crossed to Matinicus Island. His wife was an invalid, his son was away on a cruise, and his other four children were little girls. The following day it became breezy and the wind increased to a gale, and soon it developed into a storm. Before long, the seas were sweeping over the rock.

Down among the boulders was a chicken coop which Abbie feared might be carried away. On a lonely ocean outpost like Matinicus Rock, a chicken is regarded with affectionate interest, and Abbie waited her chance. When the seas fell off a little, she rushed knee-deep through the swirling water and rescued all but one of the chickens. She had hardly closed the door of the lighthouse behind her when a wave, breaking over the rock, brought down the old cobblestone chicken coop with a crash.

While the storm was at its height, the waves threatened the granite dwelling so that the family had to take refuge in the towers for safety. Here they remained, with no sound to greet them from without but the roaring of the wind around the lanterns and no sight but the sea rushing over the rock. Yet through it all, the lamps were trimmed and lighted. Even after the  storm abated, the sea between the rock and Matinicus Island was so rough that Captain Burgess could not return until four weeks later.

Afterward Abbie wrote to a friend, "Though at times greatly exhausted with my labors, not once did the lights fail."

During a subsequent winter there was so long a spell of rough weather that provisions ran low, and Captain Burgess was obliged to take the first chance of putting off for Matinicus Island, although there was no telling how soon the sea might roughen up again. In point of fact, a heavy storm broke over the coast before he could return, and before long there was danger of famine on the rock. Twenty-one days passed before he returned—days of hope alternating with fear, and the hardship of meager fare, with the daily allowance dwindling to an egg and a cup of cornmeal each, with danger of that giving out if the storm did not abate. During all this time Abbie was obliged not only to care for the lights, but also to tend an invalid mother and cheer up the little family in its desolate state.

In 1861, Captain Burgess retired from Matinicus, and a Captain Grant and his family succeeded him. Now the grim old wave-battered rock became the scene of as pretty a romance as could be devised. A son of Captain Grant had been appointed assistant to his father, and Captain Burgess had left Abbie on the rock to instruct the newcomers in the care of the lights. Young Grant proved a very apt pupil—so apt that he was soon able not only to take care of the lights, but also to persuade his instructress to let him take care of her. She became his wife and his helpmate in a double sense, for not long after their marriage she was appointed an assistant keeper.

When she was married, she had lived on the rock eight years, and she remained there until 1875, when they became the lighthouse keepers at White Head. She had performed the triple duties of wife, mother, and lighthouse keeper. The transfer to White Head brought some change from the old accustomed surroundings, but the duties, requiring such faithful performance, were the same. The Grants remained fifteen years in charge of White Head.

Shortly before leaving White Head, Mrs. Grant wrote to a friend, "Sometimes I think the time is not far distant when I shall climb these lighthouse stairs no more. It has almost seemed to me that the light was a part of myself. When we had care of the old lard-oil lamps on Matinicus Rock, they were more difficult to tend than these lamps are . . . And many nights I have watched the lights my part of the night, and then could not sleep the rest of the night, thinking nervously what might happen should the light fail.

"In all these years I always put the lamps in order in the morning, and I lit them at sunset. Those old lamps are so thoroughly impressed on my memory that even now I often dream of them. There were fourteen lamps and fourteen reflectors . . . If I ever have a gravestone, I would like it to be in the form of a lighthouse or beacon."

Abbie died in 1892, and there is a lighthouse standing guard over her grave.

Virtue Study

Memory Verse: Psalm 119:105. Write this verse on a 3 x 5 card and memorize it during the week.

1. What virtues did Abbie have?
2. How did she manage things when her father was away?

Lighthouses served as beacons for ships. They let them know of rocks and reefs as well as being guiding lights to ports. If the light went out, a ship could lose its way in the darkness and be dashed to pieces on the rocks.

In the Bible, God often refers to Himself as "light." What do these verses say about light and God?
- 2 Samuel 22:29
- 2 Corinthians 4:6
- 1 John 1:5–7

In the New Testament we are told to be a light as well. What do these verses say about that subject?
- Matthew 5:14–16
- Acts 13:47
- 1 Thessalonians 5:5–8
- 1 Peter 2:9

WEEK 7 ~ DAY 2

Princess Sarah, Part 1
By Major-General Oliver O. Howard, 1908

She's remembered as Sarah Winnemucca, but her real name was Toc-me-to-ne, which means *shell-flower*. Her people were Paiute Indians, and they lived in what is now the great state of Nevada. When she was quite a little girl, her grandfather, Chief Winnemucca, took his family and went to live in California, and when they came back she was almost grown up.

Great changes took place in the life of this Indian princess when the first group of white-topped prairie wagons came slowly toward them across the desert. Her people were filled with surprise as they saw the unusual sight.

Her grandfather and the warriors crawled to the top of a low hill and watched the "tents" rolling over the plain, drawn by "strange buffalo with long horns." For three days, they kept along with this wagon train, but the people in the train never suspected they were thus watched.

The Indians watched from a distance the passing trains of white traders. On one occasion, her Grandfather Winnemucca, after assuring the white men of his peaceable intentions, actually visited their camp. When he left them, they gave him a new tin basin. He wondered what on earth that could be for, till he saw, of course, that it must be a hat. So with great dignity he put the tin basin on his head and walked back to his people, who wondered at the beautiful headpiece and gave him a new name: "The Shining Moon."

Then the women ventured near, dragging the trembling children. Sarah remembered a horrible thing walking toward her, which later she knew was a big man with bushy black whiskers all over his face. But of course, among Indians she had never seen a beard, so when this big man took the little Indian girl by the hand, she saw only a great nose and two staring eyes, and she said she must have fainted, for that was all she remembered. But afterward her mother laughed when the little Sarah told her of the great "demon owl" that had seized her.

Her grandfather was very fond of her, so she was sad and lonesome indeed when he died, but she did not forget his last words to her before he went. "Sweetheart," he said, "do not forget my white brothers. Be kind to them, and they will be kind to you and teach you many things."

In California, the old chief gave the names Jerry, Natchez, Lee, Mary, and Sarah to his grandchildren. Sarah learned to speak fairly good English and later spent time with an American family who taught her to sew, cook, and do housework.

When Sarah was fifteen years old, she made the long, five hundred mile journey to California once more with her brothers and sister and grandmother. Her brothers took care of cattle for a good man named Mr. Scott, who had known and loved Chief Winnemucca, and he gave them good wages, several fine horses, and two ponies for Sarah and Mary to ride. The sisters had always ridden bareback like Indian men, but when Christmas came, Sarah was surprised to find a beautiful sidesaddle from her brother Lee, and she learned to ride like the white ladies and was very proud and happy.

Now, the Paiutes lived by hunting and fishing, not by farming, so they moved from place to place wherever there was game. When they were in the mountains, rough white settlers came to Pyramid Lake and caught almost all of the fish with nets so that there were no fish when the Indians returned. This made the Indians angry, and so trouble began. All this time, Sarah was in California. Her father, Chief Winnemucca the Second, and her mother were in Nevada, and she often heard good news from them, but one spring when she was seventeen years old, two Indians came bringing the news from her father that he was in the mountains and wanted all his children to come to him, but especially Sarah.

Starting on their ponies, they began the journey, riding beside the wagon where their grandmother rode. It took twenty-five days to reach Carson City, but here their father and mother met them, and the next day all went to see Governor Nye, whom Sarah told in English what her father, the chief, wanted to say.

Governor Nye was very jolly and good, and when he knew how things really were he told the white settlers not to interfere with the Indians and sent soldiers from the fort to drive the rough men away, so Governor Nye and Chief Winnemucca became good friends, as they never could have been but for little Toc-me-to-ne and her bright, intelligent speech.

For the next year, Sarah talked both Paiute and English, and settled many little troubles. She was called "friend" by the Indians, the soldiers, and her father. She thought often of old Chief Winnemucca's words and kept peace with their white brothers.

Virtue Study

Work on Psalm 119:105, the memory verse for this week.

1. How was Sarah raised?
2. What influence did the white men have on her and her family?
3. Why did her grandfather want her to look at the whites as brothers?

Her grandfather saw the value of learning. What does the Bible say about gaining knowledge and what we should learn?
- Job 34:4
- Psalm 119:73
- Proverbs 1:7–9
- Proverbs 9:9
- Proverbs 13:14
- Matthew 11:29
- Titus 3:14

Box of Visual Reminders

Make a little tepee using toothpicks, paper, and glue. Put this in your box to remind you of Sarah, of how she loved to learn, and of how she pursued peace.

WEEK 7 ~ DAY 3

Princess Sarah, Part 2
By Major-General Oliver O. Howard, 1908

Then people began to whisper that there would be war between the soldiers and the Paiutes. One day some old men were fishing in a lake when cavalry soldiers rode up and fired at them. The Indians ran to their tepees nearby, but the soldiers followed and hurt some of them. The captain of the soldiers thought they belonged to a band of bad Indians, and as he spoke only English, none could explain. As soon as they understood the cruel mistake, of course, everyone was very sorry and did what they could to make it right. One of Sarah's little sisters was badly hurt, but Chief Winnemucca and Sarah only spoke sadly of the "Lake Harney trouble" and were still friendly to the white people.

About this time Sarah came down to Muddy Lake to help her brother Natchez, who was a subchief there. Nearby, Mr. Nugent, the Indian agent, had a big store where he sold all sorts of things. Now, the government did not allow agents to sell shot and gunpowder to the Indians, but one day Mr. Nugent did sell some to a Paiute Indian. The Indian rode away across the river very happy, but soon one of Mr. Nugent's men met him. He saw the shot and powder and in English told the Indian to give them up. Of course the Indian could not understand and tried to ride on, and then the white man fired and shot him. The dreadful news spread among all the Indians, and they were very angry and said Mr. Nugent must die, because they believed he had let the Paiute have the powder and then sent his man to shoot him on his way.

Angry Indians rushed to Natchez. Frightened women and children gathered around Sarah. But they both mounted their swift ponies and hurried away to save the agent's life if possible. The river at the ford was high. Sarah's pony stumbled in the swift current and threw her off, but her brother helped her to remount, and with wet clothes, she galloped to Mr. Nugent's house. When Sarah saw him, she cried to him to get away quickly or the Indians would kill him, but he replied that he was not afraid and called his men to get their guns to fight the Indians.

Natchez and Sarah begged him to go away till they could quiet the angry Indians, but he would not, and he told them to leave him. There was nothing else to do, but at the ford they met the angry Indians and stopped them. Natchez called a council in his tepee, and here he and Sarah succeeded in stopping the Indians. Soon afterward, word came that two white men herding horses near a place called

Deep Wells had been shot by the brothers of the Paiute Indian who bought the powder. Then Mr. Nugent sent for soldiers to punish the Indians.

Now, when the agent asked for soldiers, Captain Jerome—who was a wise man—decided to know the truth first, so he sent two friendly Indians with a letter to Sarah. He wrote: "Miss Sarah Winnemucca, your agent tells us very bad things about your people killing two of our men. I want you and your brother Natchez to meet me at my place tonight. I want to talk to you and your brother."

The Indians were terrified when Sarah told them what was in the letter and said, "Write, write, you may be able to save us from a dreadful war." Sarah had nothing to write with, but she said, "I will try."

With a sharp-pointed stick and some fish blood, she scratched off this letter: "Honorable Sir, my brother is not here. I am looking for him every minute. We will go as soon as he comes in. If he comes tonight, we will come sometime late in the night. Yours truly, Sarah Winnemucca."

The messengers were hardly gone when Natchez and his men returned. They took fresh horses, and he and Sarah started for the fort. She says, "We went like the wind, never stopping till we got there."

When they arrived, the wicked agent was with Captain Jerome, but Sarah told the whole story, and the Captain treated them well and promised to do what was right. Then the brother and sister, tired as they were, rode back to their tepee on Muddy Lake. The next day a good officer and some soldiers came and camped near them. The soldiers gave the Indians food and stood guard while Sarah and Natchez held meetings with their people and showed them how kind the soldiers had been. After this, because of the bad ways of Nugent, the commander at Fort McDermit had Natchez and many Indians come to the army post and pitch their tepees. Sarah lived with her brother and his wife, and was the interpreter and peacemaker; and she persuaded the chief, her father, to get together as many as possible of the wandering Paiutes and bring them to the fort.

Virtue Study

Work on Psalm 119:105, the memory verse for this week.

1. What did Sarah do to prevent a war?
2. What virtues did she have?
3. Why did she try so hard to preserve peace?

What does the Bible say about peacemakers and those who pursue peace?
- ♥ Psalm 119:165
- ♥ Proverbs 12:20
- ♥ Isaiah 32:17
- ♥ Romans 12:17–21
- ♥ 2 Corinthians 13:11
- ♥ Ephesians 4:3
- ♥ 1 Thessalonians 5:13b

Who gives peace?
- ♥ Psalm 29:11

WEEK 7 ~ DAY 4

Princess Sarah, Part 3
By Major-General Oliver O. Howard, 1908

It was in 1878 that the Bannock Indians started on the warpath in Idaho, and joining the Malheur Paiutes, fought the white people wherever they went. This was called the Bannock War. The princess, Sarah Winnemucca, was riding near Fort Lyons, Idaho, when she heard of the trouble. She was on her way to a railway station at Elko, Nevada, hoping to go to Washington to try to have some wrongs by the Malheur agency corrected.

When she heard the news, she at once turned back and went to the sheep ranch near Boise City, and when Major-General Oliver O. Howard heard she was there, he telegraphed to Captain Bernard, who was nearby with some soldiers, to ask the "princess" to go as a messenger of peace to the angry Indians. She said she would go, and taking with her some true Indian friends, rode over one hundred miles in a day and a half. She was approaching the Indian camp in the dark and wondering how to get in unnoticed when she heard a sound. She called, and an answering sign showed her it was an Indian. To her surprise and delight, it proved to be her own brother, Lee Winnemucca.

They had a long talk, and Sarah changed her usual neat dress for an old skirt and Indian blanket, painting her face and pulling a shawl over her head like the squaws. Then she went straight into the Indian camp and to her father's lodge among the fighting warriors, who never thought for a moment of why she was there. When she saw her father, she had a long talk with him in the Paiute language and begged him not to have war with his white brothers.

When she returned to the American camp, she told General Howard her story. "I took my brother's blanket and dressed as a squaw. I painted my face. When we came near the camp, there were a great, great many people and horses. I was afraid. But I went to my father's camp and talked with my people. I told them the soldiers were coming. They said they were really held prisoners by the Bannocks, and could not come away. I told them they must. 'Here,' said I, 'go hide your ponies in the bushes, and after dark you can leave.' My brother Lee got a pony for me. After dark we slipped out, a few at a time, and stole away. We all agreed to meet at a certain place.

"Lee and my father and I went out with about fifteen others. We journeyed all night. At daylight our horses were worn out, and we stopped at the place of meeting. Presently a man came up just as fast as he could and said my brother Jerry and some others of the last had been discovered and pursued; that he had heard much firing and feared all were killed. Then the women began weeping and moaning, and all was trouble. My brother Lee said, 'I will go back and die with my people.'

"My father and I called to him, but he jumped on his horse and went. He blamed me for being the cause of all this and said I had brought nothing but trouble on them. Then my father started to go back. 'For,' said he, 'my son will be killed, then why should I live?' Then said I to him, 'You must not go back, here are women and children depending on you!' Then he waved his hand and said, 'What shall we do? If we try to go away, the Bannocks will kill us. If we stay, the soldiers will kill us.' Then he said to me, 'Sarah, go to the soldiers. Tell them where we are, and that if they do not hurry we shall be killed. Tell them to come to us, come at once. Spare not your horse, Sarah, but ride night and day.' Then I left him. Mattie" (her sister-in-law) "and I came just as fast as ever our horses could travel. Oh, I am afraid they are all killed! There was only one gun among them. My father said, 'Come at once.' Why do you wait?"

Sarah implored the American general to go at once to the aid of her father. Mattie stood behind her, listening intently, and seemed much frightened.

The refugees were not killed, however, but were brought back to the U.S. camp in safety. Sarah and her sister-in-law remained with the troops. Sarah acted as guide and interpreter and scout. The two women had their own tent, cared for their horses themselves, and helped at the kitchen fire and the mess table. They rode at the head of the scouts or went off alone on dangerous rides, bringing back valuable information. Not only did they read the trail as an open book, but they knew the Indian character so well that they would foretell the line of march and future plans of the enemy. When prisoners were taken, Sarah was of great assistance as interpreter, and by spreading her influence induced many to surrender. At the close of the campaign, Sarah accompanied the prisoners of war to their new home on a reservation.

Sarah was sweet and handsome and very quick and able. When she grew older, she married one of the young army officers, but later he went east and she lived on the Malheur Indian Reservation. Here she was always called "the princess" because of her influence over her people. By her tireless perseverance, she finally succeeded in getting permission for her tribe to return to their former homes.

She did the United States great service, and if a tenth of all she willingly did to help the white settlers and her own people to live peacefully together were told, the name of Toc-me-to-ne would have a prominent place beside the name of Pocahontas in the history of our country.

Virtue Study

Work on Psalm 119:105, the memory verse for this week.

1. How did Sarah help end the Bannock War?
2. What did she do to help her people after the war?
3. How was she a spokeswoman for her people?
4. Sarah displayed a lot of virtues. What are some of them?

If Sarah had a life verse, what do you think it would be? Have fun looking up different verses that talk about our purpose on earth.

Does Sarah remind you of anyone in the Bible? Read 1 Samuel 25 and Esther for some examples.

Sarah's peacemaking skills helped save many lives. Read 1 Samuel 25 and answer these questions:
- ♥ What did Abigail do when she heard of David's request?
- ♥ How did she persuade David to change his mind?
- ♥ What visual picture did she use in verse 29?
- ♥ How did Abigail's story end?

WEEK 7 ~ DAY 5

The Compassionate Nurse, Part 1
By Clayton Edwards, 1920

As the name of Florence Nightingale became world famous at the close of the Crimean War, the name of another English nurse who suffered martyrdom in World War I will go down in history with the luster of glory and self-sacrifice surrounding it. That name is Edith Cavell.

Edith Cavell was born in Norwich, England, in 1865. Her father was an English minister who was the rector of a single parish in Norwich for more than half a century. Edith and her sister were brought up by Christian parents who taught them the value of leading useful lives and the glory of self-sacrifice. As was customary at the time, when she was a young girl, she received her education on the continent, attending school in the city of Brussels in Belgium. She then returned to her home and remained there until, when twenty-one years old and resolved to give her life to some useful and compassionate occupation, she decided to become a trained nurse and went to London to study that calling.

She studied at the London Hospital, where the hardest and most difficult conditions prevailed and where the nurses were worked to the limit of their strength. She also held the position of a nurse in two other hospitals—the Shoreditch Infirmary in Hoxton and the St. Pancras Infirmary. She gained a reputation both for hard work and effectiveness, and her patients often spoke of her gentleness and her kindness. Not content to forget a patient when he was discharged from the hospital, Edith Cavell often followed him to his home and continued there the lighter nursing that would assure his recovery. Her regular duties were severe enough, but she used a large part of her scanty leisure for such purposes as these.

In 1906, Edith Cavell left the English hospitals, where she had made a reputation for herself, and went back to Brussels, where she took a position as matron in a medical and surgical home. Nursing in Brussels had been conducted hitherto by Roman Catholic Sisters of Mercy, and at first they were inclined to look upon Miss Cavell as an untrained outsider, but her tact and skill soon won the hearts of these good women, who afforded her every courtesy.

Her home succeeded so well that three years after its beginning, Miss Cavell started a training school for nurses. She was popular everywhere in the Belgian capital, and although Protestant, she gained the praise of the Roman Catholic priests for the generous and unselfish work that she performed.

When World War I broke out, Miss Cavell was on a vacation with her mother. Twice every year she returned to England to visit her family. Her father had died by this time, but her mother was close to her heart, and she saw her as often as she could.

"I may be looked on as an old maid," she is reported as saying, "but with my work and my mother I am a very happy one, and desire nothing more as long as I have these two."

When war was declared, Miss Cavell lost no time in hurrying back to Brussels, believing that her duty called her there. She wrote a letter commenting on the German army when it swept through Belgium—and in it she voiced her pity for the tired, footsore German soldiers who were later to slay her.

Brussels soon became a part of the German Empire, and a tyrannical governor came there to establish his headquarters, issuing proclamations threatening the Belgians with death for minor offenses and filling Brussels with spies. Miss Cavell desired to continue her hospital work and went to the Governor, von Bissing, to get permission to do so. He granted it, for the quiet English nurse made an impression upon him. We are told that the arrogant German formed a high opinion of her—so much so that he secretly determined to keep her under the strictest supervision!

From that time on, spies followed her tracks. She cared for the wounded German soldiers and nursed a number of German officers as well as the Belgians who were in her care, but this made no difference to the authorities. They were determined to detect her in some crime and punish her. It was not fitting, they thought, that an enemy should be engaged in works of mercy, even though they themselves might benefit thereby.

Soon spies began to come to the governor with tales and falsehoods of the crimes that she had been committing in their eyes. They bore witness that she had given an overcoat to a Frenchman who was cold and hungry—and the Frenchman later escaped over the Dutch frontier. Once she gave a glass of water to a Belgian soldier. She had given money to poor people, perhaps to soldiers. But the main reason that the Germans hated her was because she was held in admiration by the people of Brussels.

On the night of August 5, 1915, Miss Cavell was tying up the wounds of a German soldier when a group of armed men entered the room and their leader told her roughly that she was under arrest. A blow was the only response when she tried to protest. She was taken to prison and placed in solitary confinement. Her arrest was masked with the most careful secrecy, for the Germans did not want to have the representatives of neutral governments, such as the United States, know of the affair.

Virtue Study

Recite Psalm 119:105, the memory verse for this week.

1. How does a person live a useful life?
2. How did Edith pursue the "glory of self-sacrifice"?
3. What events happened that changed Edith's life?

When the war began, Edith immediately went back to her work. God often asks people to go into difficult situations to be a light for Him. What do these verses say about that?
- ♥ Esther 4:12–17
- ♥ Acts 20:22–24

Edith had many virtues. What do these verses say about being righteous?
- ♥ Job 17:9
- ♥ Psalm 11:7
- ♥ Matthew 13:43
- ♥ 1 John 3:7

WEEK 8 ~ DAY 1

The Compassionate Nurse, Part 2
By Clayton Edwards, 1920

Word of Edith's plight did reach England through a traveler, and at once the British government requested the American ambassador, Dr. Page, to get what information he could from Mr. Whitlock, the American minister in Belgium. He went at once to the German authorities, but they avoided his questions and waited ten days before giving him a reply. Then the Germans sent him a statement declaring that Edith Cavell herself had admitted giving money to English and Belgian soldiers and furnishing them with guides to help them to the Dutch frontier, whence they might escape into Holland and return to England.

If what they said were true, there was still no cause for killing the unfortunate woman in their power, for she was not accused at any time of having been a spy. But they planned to give her a death sentence, and Mr. Whitlock soon guessed this, in spite of the fact that the Germans kept their preparations from him so far as possible.

An American lawyer, Mr. de Leval, was requested by Mr. Whitlock to take Miss Cavell's case and do whatever was possible on her behalf. He was not allowed to see the prisoner—and was not even allowed to look at the documents in the case until the trial began.

Another lawyer, who was a Belgian, suddenly appeared and told the Americans that there was not the least cause for them to worry as Miss Cavell was sure to receive only just treatment. He also promised to let them know when the trial was to take place and that he would keep them informed of all the developments in the case. All these promises were broken. It is true that he sent a note a few days before the trial telling Mr. Whitlock that the case was about to come to court, but that is all that he told them. He never informed them that the death sentence had been imposed. He never came to see them afterward. And when they sought him for an explanation, he had disappeared.

Miss Cavell was kept in solitary confinement for two months and then was tried with a number of other persons who were accused of crimes against the Germans. It was only from a private source that Mr. de Leval learned that the trial was underway and that the death sentence had been given. Miss Cavell herself, we are told, was calm, dignified, and brave at the trial and faced her accusers heroically. She was dressed in her nurse's uniform and wore the badge of the Red Cross.

When Mr. Whitlock learned that she had been tried and sentenced to death, he did everything possible to secure her pardon, or at least a moderation of the punishment. He wrote to Baron von der Lancken, pointing out in a clear and decisive manner that Miss Cavell had served the Germans by caring for their wounded and that the death sentence had never before been inflicted for the crime of which she was accused.

All through the day the American legation sent message after message to the German authorities asking for information. They received none. At 6:20 in the evening, they were told by a subordinate that the sentence had not been given—only to learn later that it had indeed been declared, and that Miss Cavell would face a firing squad at two o'clock the following morning. Mr. Whitlock then urged Baron von der Lancken to appeal to General von Bissing to lessen the sentence, and at eleven in the evening he was told that von Bissing refused to do anything to save Miss Cavell's life.

At the same time that the governor denied this appeal, Edith Cavell was allowed to see a British chaplain. She told him that she was not in the least afraid of death and willingly gave her life for her country. She said, "I have no fear nor shrinking. I have seen death so often that it is not strange or fearful to me. I thank God for this ten weeks' quiet before the end. Life has always been hurried and full of difficulty. This time of rest has been a great mercy. They have all been very kind to me. But this I would say, standing as I do in view of God and eternity, I realize that patriotism is not enough. I must have no hatred or bitterness toward anyone."

EDITH CAVELL'S EXECUTION

She then repeated the hymn ending:
"Hold thou Thy cross before my closing eyes;
Shine through the gloom and point me to the skies:
Heaven's morning breaks, and earth's vain shadows flee;
In life, in death, O Lord, abide with me."

Early in the morning, with her eyes bandaged, Miss Cavell was led out to face the rifles of the Germans. She wore an English flag over her bosom. Only Germans were witnesses of the execution, but the German chaplain who attended said that she died like a heroine.

When her death became known, the entire civilized world was shocked and horrified. In England, this murder did more to stimulate recruiting than anything else up to that time. All day long lines of men waited to sign the papers of enlistment, and in Miss Cavell's hometown every eligible man was sworn into the army.

Virtue Study

Memory Verse: Galatians 2:20. Write this verse on a 3 x 5 card and memorize it during the week.

1. What virtues did Edith have?
2. How did she see her imprisonment as a blessing?
3. How did she spend her last few weeks on earth?

How was she able to forgive those who were going to kill her? What do these verses say about that?
- ♥ Proverbs 3:25–26
- ♥ Matthew 5:43–46 and 18:21–35
- ♥ Luke 23:32–34
- ♥ Acts 7:59–60

WEEK 8 ~ DAY 2

Captured by Indians, Part 1
By Albert Franklin Blaisdell, 1922

During the colonial period in a lonely valley in southern Pennsylvania lived a man named Paul Leininger. He had a wife and four children. George, the oldest, was a young man of twenty. Barbara was twelve, Regina was ten, and the youngest boy was five or six. There was also a big watchdog named Nero.

On a frosty morning late in October 1755, Mr. Leininger read the morning lesson from the large family Bible. Then they all knelt in prayer. The good man prayed, "We thank thee, O Lord, for thy good care and love to us. Help us to live aright. We pray thee to keep us this day from harm and danger. But not our will but thine be done."

After breakfast, they made their plans for the day. Mrs. Leininger and the little boy were to go to the mill to get flour. Mr. Leininger and George were to work in the field. The two girls, Barbara and Regina, were to stay in the cabin and keep house with Nero. The little boy sat before his mother on the horse. When they were passing by the field, he waved his little hand and called out, "Goodbye, Papa; goodbye, George."

Barbara was busy all morning. At noon, she blew a blast on the old tin horn to call her father and brother to dinner. While they were eating, Nero dashed in. The old dog was greatly excited. His hair stood up, and he growled fiercely.

Mr. Leininger knew that the faithful dog would not run from any common foe. He left the table and went to the cabin door.

Bang, came a sharp crack from a rifle, and he fell dead on the floor.

George sprang to help his father. *Bang,* came another rifle shot, and he too fell dead.

A moment later, a dozen yelling Indians rushed into the cabin. Nero leaped at the throat of a man, only to be killed by a tomahawk. Barbara hid in the loft. Poor little Regina knelt and began to pray.

The Indians ate the dinner which the girls had made ready for their father and brother. Then they began to plunder the cabin. They dragged Barbara from her hiding place, set fire to the cabin, and took the two girls into the woods.

"Oh, Mamma, Mamma! Oh, where is my mother?" the girls heard someone call as they were dragged along. The cry came from a little girl tied to a tree. Her name was Susie Smith. Her father and mother, who lived near, had been killed a few hours before.

The warriors now carried the three girls into the deep woods. What a sad homecoming was that for the good wife and mother in the evening!

"We must surely have taken the wrong trail," said Mrs. Leininger to herself.

No, there was the big pine tree that stood near their house. But no cabin was to be seen. The rising smoke told the sad story.

The poor mother began to understand the awful truth that her family had been killed or carried away by the Indians. She fell on her knees and sobbed a prayer to God for help.

How sad and terrible was the grief of the poor woman during the long years that followed! She tried to learn of the fate of her children, but she could not discover anything about them. Kindhearted friends built her a log cabin where she lived with her young son, who was now her only comfort.

The three little girls, Regina, Barbara, and Susie, were taken deep into the woods.

For many days the Indians and the children tramped through the woods. After a time they came to an Indian village.

Virtue Study

Work on Galatians 2:20, the memory verse for this week.

1. Read Mr. Leininger's prayer again. What did he pray for? How did he end the prayer?
2. How much faith did the Leininger family have?

Read Matthew 26:36–44. What does Jesus ask His Father to do? How does He finish His prayer?

In Philippians 4:6, Paul gives us a good description of how to pray. God always answers prayer, but sometimes the answer is no.

How can you learn to finish your prayers with the same kind of surrender, "Not my will but thine be done," that Jesus and Mr. Leininger did?

Read Matthew 6:9–13. What does it say in verse 10?

WEEK 8 ~ DAY 3

Captured by Indians, Part 2
By Albert Franklin Blaisdell, 1922

Barbara was sent to a different village and managed to escape. An old Indian squaw took the other two girls as her own children. Regina was given a long Indian name which meant "the White Lily."

The old squaw had a longer name meaning "the Dark and Rainy Cloud." It was a good name for her, for she was often cross and unkind to the girls, and would beat them.

Regina and Susie's life for the next ten years was hard and lonely. As the time passed by, Regina learned to speak the Indian language and almost forgot her own.

She used to go alone into the woods. Here she would repeat the Lord's Prayer, which her good mother had taught her in their cabin home. She would sing some of the hymns she had learned when a little girl. One of the hymns began:

"Alone, and yet not all alone am I
In this lone wilderness."

Little by little she forgot how the log cabin in the woods looked. The face of her dear mother and the happy children about the fireplace seemed like a dream. Even the awful scene of that last day slowly faded from her memory.

Sometime later, Colonel Henry Bouquet, a British officer, drove the Indians across the Ohio River and compelled them to give up their captives.

These captives were brought to Fort Pitt, where Pittsburgh now stands. Fathers and mothers came from far and near to see if they could find their long-lost children. It was a joyful but a sad and pathetic sight. The old Indian fighters shed tears when they saw the mothers crying over their dear ones.

But fifty or more of the children had nobody to claim them. Among these was White Lily. Poor Mrs. Leininger had nearly lost hope that God would answer her prayers and send her tidings of her children. All these long years, she had sung at evening time her favorite hymn:

"Alone, and yet not all alone am I
In this lone wilderness."

Tears would run down her wrinkled cheeks as she thought how many times she had sung the old hymn to her little ones in the days of long ago.

"Come to Carlisle about the middle of September, my dear Mrs. Leininger," said Colonel Bouquet to her. "Many lost children will be brought there. Perhaps yours will be with them."

The poor old mother left her cabin in the mountains and went to Carlisle. The unclaimed children stood in a line as the anxious fathers and mothers passed along, trying to pick out their dear lost ones.

The careworn Mrs. Leininger looked into the faces of the girls, hoping to find her daughters. It was in vain. Crying as if her heart would break, she made ready to go back to her home.

"Can you not find your children, Mrs. Leininger?" asked the British officer.

"No, indeed, sir," she replied, "they are not here."

"Are you sure? Are there no signs or marks by which you might know them?"

"No, Colonel, there was not even a scar."

"My good woman, surely you used to sing to your little girls. Is there no song they loved? Sing to these young folks one of the songs you used to sing to your children when they were little."

"I used to sing them to sleep with an old hymn. But these soldiers will laugh at me if I sing."

"Try it, while I walk along the line and watch for you."

The old mother took heart. She began to sing, in a clear but trembling voice, the dear old hymn of her cabin home:

"Alone, and yet not all alone am I

In this lone wilderness."

Men, women, and children became silent and turned to look and listen. The faithful old mother stood with closed eyes. Her hands were clasped. The sun lighted up her wrinkled face and her snow-white hair.

When she began the second verse of the hymn, a tall, Indian-like girl ran to her. She threw her arms about her neck and sobbed, "Mother, Mother!"

Almost in a faint, the aged mother cried, "Oh, my God, it is Regina, my dear little girl!"

Regina joined her mother in singing again the old hymn:

"Alone, and yet not all alone am I

In this lone wilderness."

Virtue Study

Work on Galatians 2:20, the memory verse for this week.

1. What did Regina do to remind herself of her home and God?
2. How was Regina reunited with her mother?

Regina must have felt forsaken at times. Who felt forsaken in these verses?
- Psalm 22:1–31
- Mark 15:34

What do these verses say about not being forsaken?
- Psalm 9:10
- Psalm 37:25

Ten years is a long time, and no doubt Regina sometimes felt like God had abandoned her. What does God's Word say about that?
- Psalm 94:14
- Isaiah 41:10
- Hebrews 13:5b

Read the hymns on the next two pages. The original was written in German, and Regina would have sung it in that language.

Act out this story.

Alone, and Yet Not Alone Am I
Version 1
By Benjamin Schmolk, 1672-1737

Alone, and yet not alone am I,
Though in this solitude so drear;
I feel my Savior always nigh,
He comes the weary hour to cheer:
I am with Him and He with me,
E'en here alone I cannot be!

Alone, and yet not all alone am I
In this lone wilderness.
I feel my Savior always nigh;
He comes the weary hours to bless.
I am with Him, and He with me,
E'en here alone I cannot be.

Alone, and yet not all alone am I
In this great loneliness;
When I my solitude bemoan,
God cheers the hours of my distress.
I am with Him and He with me,
I fear no lonely destiny.

Alone, and Yet Not Alone Am I
Version 2
By Benjamin Schmolk, 1672-1737

I am alone, yet not alone,
For Thou art near:
I cannot see Thy loving face,
But I can hear
The cheering promise of Thy grace.

Thou wilt not leave me in the dark
When falls the night;
For round my path and in my soul
Thou art the Light
To guide me with Thy sweet control.

No want can steal my rich supplies
Of love and peace;
For though I lack what others hold,
My stores increase
With heavenly gifts more rare than gold.

And Thou wilt bear me all life through,
And in the end
Wilt still abide what Thou hast been,
My constant Friend,
And take me where Thy face is seen.

WEEK 8 ~ DAY 4

The Warrior Mother, Part 1
By Mrs. Octavius Freire Owen, 1854

Jane de Montfort thoughtfully rocked the cradle where her little baby slept. She hardly seemed to hear the voices of the lords who gathered around her.

"Countess," one of the bolder nobles said, "did you understand what we told you?"

Her reply came with effort. "Yes, you said that my husband has been captured by his enemies and taken to Paris, and is even now shut up in a tower of the Louvre. My poor John!" Her sadness seemed to sweep into the corners of the room like a strong wind, but then she lifted her head a little and said, "Charles de Blois will stop at nothing to take over the land that rightly belongs to my husband and my son."

Something seemed to rise in the bosom of the countess; her beautiful face was suddenly bright with purpose and determination. She would not let her husband's property in Brittany be stolen. Their son was the heir, and she would save it for him till he was grown.

"My lords," she said to the nobles gathered in her castle, "assemble the people in Rennes. I shall continue the war against King Philip in place of my husband."

Doubt showed on the faces of the lords. Could Jane de Montfort, one of the most beautiful women of the age, have any knowledge or skill in war? Her bold face full of purpose told them not to question her. Instead, they went out and did as she said.

During the dark days of the Middle Ages, the countries of France and England were constantly at war. This war lasted such a long time that it has become known as the Hundred Years' War. Jane de Montfort lived during the beginning of this war in the 1300s.

Several days later, bearing her babe in her arms, she presented herself before the people of Rennes and eloquently set forth the claims of her tiny child. She enlisted the hearts of her hearers in the struggle to support his interests. With appeals, Jane mingled clever suggestions respecting the freedom of Brittany, which she represented as likely to be sacrificed to the king of France if they failed.

From fortress to fortress this heroic

woman journeyed, encouraging the wavering, planning with the powerful, arranging for all—and everywhere with the same success. Finally, having spared no effort to put her followers in fair order of defense, she shut herself within the town of Hennebon and awaited the approach of the hostile troops.

The countess knew she could never be victorious alone, and therefore she sent a request to the king of England, Edward III. She suggested that her baby son should be betrothed to one of Edward's young daughters. This agreement would include Edward sending aid to the countess.

Before a response could arrive from the English king, Charles de Blois arrived with an immense train of soldiers at the town of Rennes. In a short time, the countess had the humiliation of hearing that it had surrendered. Scarcely had these tidings reached her when they were followed up by the rapid advance of the French army, and Jane found herself blockaded within the walls of her fortress.

Countess de Montfort was always on the alert, always present to give an encouraging word to the troops, always on hand to advise the nobles, and always convinced that victory would be hers. So well organized were her plans, so well disciplined her soldiers, that no advantage could be gained from without. Riding up and down the streets, the female general, clothed in complete armor, urged bravery upon her hearers, incited all who could hold a sword to the combat, and summoned even women and children to the fray, employing them in hurling stones and missiles upon the besiegers.

It would be difficult to overrate the effect which this dauntless and personal enthusiasm produced. Few men sat a horse better than this princess; in combat she handled the sword with as much address and effect as the most vigorous warriors.

Nature, which had endowed her with an elegant form and beautiful features, spoke all the louder in her cause when it was seen she knew how to forgo the privileges of her gender to share the hardships of the lowest trooper while she assumed the entire responsibility of the camp. Frequent sallies headed by herself were made, and they were rewarded with constant success.

On one occasion, having observed that the assailants had forgotten to guard a distant post, she hurried forth, accompanied by only two hundred horsemen, threw them into disorder, and after doing great damage to their ranks, set fire to their tents and baggage. In the enthusiasm of the fight, she had forgotten that she might be unable to return in safety. A considerable force now lay between her little band and the gates of the town. The inhabitants saw her position with unspeakable dread. Only a few moments were necessary to arrange her plans: she gave the word for her men to disband and to make their way to Brest.

Virtue Study

Work on Galatians 2:20, the memory verse for this week.

1. Why did Jane become a warrior?
2. What did she do to protect her son's inheritance?
3. What were some of her virtues?

Jane was willing to endure great hardship to fight for her son's inheritance. Mothers often have a special gift of self-sacrifice. Read Ruth 1–4. How did Naomi care for her daughter-in-law?

How did Jane de Montfort demonstrate the characteristics mentioned in Proverbs 31:10–31?

WEEK 8 ~ DAY 5

The Warrior Mother, Part 2
By Mrs. Octavius Freire Owen, 1854

At Brest, Jane met the soldiers at the appointed rendezvous, bringing with her a force of five hundred more cavalry soldiers, and headed toward Hennebon. She broke through the enemy's lines and was reunited with her disheartened friends (who had mourned her for lost)—unhurt and in great triumph. She was received with every token of rejoicing. Trumpets pealed and acclamations rent the air, disturbing the troops without, who hastily armed themselves while those inside the town mounted the walls to defend it. The contest lasted until past noon. Vast numbers of the besiegers were killed, and their leader at length decided upon retiring to attack the castle of Auray, leaving Sir Herve de Leon to annoy and vex the garrison, for which purpose he sent twelve large machines to cast stones by which to destroy the castle.

The siege lasted a long time, and no help from England came. Many began to say that they would never come and that sooner or later the enemy would break through the wall.

Jane often watched for the ships from the top of a tower. One day, her lady-in-waiting approached her as she stood at her post.

"Countess, have you heard what the bishop of Leon is saying?"

Jane did not seem to hear the maid, but a breeze from the sea found her hair and tugged at it. Then she replied, more to the sea than to the maid, "Enemies without and enemies within, and still the English delay."

Her maid answered, "Surely you could bring the nobles who have been listening to the lies of the bishop to stop this talk of surrender."

A large group of nobles had gathered in the great hall of the castle and they were talking excitedly. The bishop of Leon had persuaded many of them to surrender by offering safety: his nephew was Sir Herve de Leon, and the bishop promised to save all those who would help bring peace. Suddenly the countess appeared, dressed in her armor. Her very presence stopped the excited prattle. Her intense eyes roamed around the room and at last fell on the face of the bishop.

"What has Sir Herve de Leon offered you for your service in delivering this city to him?" The countess was a woman of deep insight and she saw through this scheme. "Surely, your nephew will reward you gallantly for helping to bring a victory to the French. I for one would be interested to know what promises he has made to you, that you would so discourage the nobles from the current struggle."

The bishop at first was taken off guard, but he soon recovered and replied, "I do not know what you mean, madam. My interest is merely for the poor people in this sad city who will perish if we do not surrender soon."

His clever answer seemed to impress the nobles, but the countess did not seem pleased and she firmly said, "The English will arrive soon." Then she reminded them of all the things that her family had suffered and how they should not abandon her in her time of need. After her diplomatic speech, she left the room.

Back on the tower, she eagerly watched for the ships that should be coming from England. She heard a commotion in the court below and saw the nobles walking toward the gate. It was over now. She could see that the bishop had won and the nobles were going to surrender the city. The sad moment had arrived when all her brave plans were to be abandoned. Perhaps she would be dragged to prison with her child for whom she was fighting. In despair, she scanned the sea again, knowing that the ocean would be empty just as it was a few seconds ago. But wait! Could it be? She rushed to the nobles and shouted with joy, "I see ships! I see the English vessels! No surrender!"

Joyously, the besieged and worn townspeople ran to the ramparts. The good tidings were confirmed, and happiness again shone upon the faces of the lately complaining garrison. The English forces, headed by Sir Walter de Manny, entered the town and were enthusiastically received by the lady and her soldiers, the treacherous bishop having taken himself off.

Some months after this, a truce of peace was to be observed until the following summer. The countess paid a visit to the English court, where she met the princess who was to become her son's wife. She also hoped to arrange some plan for the delivery of her husband.

Obtaining further assistance from King Edward, she embarked on her homeward journey. With the help of the English, they took Vannes. Later, King Edward determined to go in person to the assistance of his fair ally. But his presence didn't bring about any favorable results, and his enterprise was concluded by a somewhat compromising treaty.

Jane's husband managed to escape, but he died shortly afterward. Till her son came of age, she protected his inheritance. In her old age, she retired to the Chateau of Lucinio, near Vannes, where the remainder of her life was spent in comparative quiet. Her son inherited her brave and dauntless spirit and was known as John the Valiant.

Virtue Study

Recite Galatians 2:20, the memory verse for this week.

1. How did the countess handle the enemy within her castle?
2. What did she do while she was waiting for help to arrive?
3. What would have happened if she hadn't been watching for the ships?
4. What should we do while we are waiting (be it for dinner, a doctor's appointment, or direction from God)?

Read these verses. What does God says about waiting?
- ♥ Psalm 5:3
- ♥ Psalm 33:20
- ♥ Psalm 37:7
- ♥ Psalm 130:5–6
- ♥ Proverbs 20:22
- ♥ Isaiah 30:18
- ♥ Micah 7:7
- ♥ Hebrews 9:28
- ♥ Jude 1:21

WEEK 9 ~ DAY 1

The Valiant Maid of Orleans, Part 1
By Anna H. Carter, 1914

The story of Joan of Arc (known in French as Jeanne d'Arc) is so unusual and so wonderful that it would be difficult to believe it to be true if all that happened to her had not been told in a court of law and written down during her lifetime.

Joan was born sometime between 1410 and 1412 in the little village of Domremy, France, being the fifth child of Jacques and Isabelle d'Arc. Her parents were peasants in comfortable circumstances, and Joan did not suffer through poverty. She never learned to read or write—indeed, very few people at that time were able to do so—but she became skillful in the use of the needle and helped her mother in all the household tasks. She was always good and obedient to her parents and kind to everyone, especially the sick and the poor.

When work for the day was over, Joan ran about with her playmates, full of fun and frolic, dancing and singing for the pure joy of living. Often the children would run to the beautiful forest near the village where they played. Joan would sometimes steal away from her companions and sit quietly and thoughtfully by herself. For she lived in a very unhappy time. Her father had told her of the sad condition of France, of how the kings of England had been for nearly a hundred years trying to make themselves kings of France, and how, little by little, they had taken possession of French lands until it was feared they would soon own the entire country and France would have an English king. Charles, called the Dauphin, son of the old French king, did not dare to be crowned, and no prince was thought to be king of France until that ceremony had taken place. For centuries, the French kings had been crowned and anointed with oil at the Cathedral of Rheims, but as the city of Rheims was far away and in the power of the English, Charles thought he could not safely go there.

As Joan grew older, she spent much of her time alone and in prayer, brooding over the wrongs of her country. She implored God to have pity on France. Although she was only a young, uneducated country girl, who could neither ride a horse nor use a sword, she felt that God wanted her to rescue France by helping crown the Dauphin.

When she told her father and mother what she intended to do, they tried to discourage her, telling her that it was impossible for a girl to do what trained military men and great generals had failed to accomplish. Though it was very hard for her to act contrary to the wishes of her parents, Joan said she must do the work God had planned for her. Soon her gentle persistence had its effect, and people stopped laughing at her. Indeed, some even began to believe in her mission.

Joan would go to the Dauphin, who was then living at Chinon, a castle on the Loire, and tell him that she had come to lead his army to victory and that he would soon go to Rheims to be crowned.

At first it seemed impossible for her to get to Chinon, but she went to Vaucouleurs, where her uncle lived, and with his help she

succeeded in persuading Robert de Baudricourt, the commander there, to give her an escort of a few armed men for the journey. Someone gave her a beautiful warhorse, which, to the surprise of all, she rode well—though she had never ridden before in her life. She cut her beautiful black hair short and dressed herself in a doublet and hose. This costume she wore during the remainder of her life.

On February 23, 1429, she rode out of Vaucouleurs through a gate which is still standing, and after several days' journey came to Chinon. The Dauphin in his castle of Chinon had no such brave spirit as Joan's and was more interested in getting what pleasure he could out of his poor surroundings than in fighting his way to Rheims to be crowned. He was surrounded by men who cared nothing for the Dauphin's real interests and who persuaded him to believe it would be useless to try to oppose the English.

When Joan of Arc reached the place, she sent a messenger to the castle with a request to see and speak privately with the Dauphin.

"Why should you waste your time on a peasant maid?" asked his foolish advisers. "If she has a message, it can be given to someone else. Send someone to receive the message, sire, and spare yourself the weariness of a personal interview. She is probably some insane person who only imagines she has something of importance to tell you."

Virtue Study

Memory Verse: Ephesians 6:10–11. Write this verse on a 3 x 5 card and memorize it during the week.

1. Why was Joan's heart heavy?
2. What did she decide to do?
3. How did she overcome difficulties?

What do these verses say about overcoming?
- ♥ Jeremiah 1:19
- ♥ John 16:33
- ♥ Romans 12:21
- ♥ 1 John 4:4
- ♥ 1 John 5:3–4

The Bible often refers to the Christian walk as a battle and those who follow Christ as soldiers. What do these verses say about that?
- ♥ 2 Corinthians 10:3–4
- ♥ 1 Timothy 6:12
- ♥ 2 Timothy 2:3–4
- ♥ 1 Peter 5:8

WEEK 9 ~ DAY 2

The Valiant Maid of Orleans, Part 2
By Anna H. Carter, 1914

At the urging of his advisers, the Dauphin sent great men of his household to be entrusted with her messages. To these men the maid gently but firmly refused to speak. "God has sent me to the Dauphin, and to no one else," said she. "Tell him there is no time to lose. In proof that I speak the truth, if the Dauphin will only grant me an interview, tell him I shall recognize him, however carefully he may be disguised."

Joan's gracious manner, her pleasant tones, and her quiet confidence made a deep impression upon the king's officers. Still they could not understand why a country maid should refuse to let them act as her messengers to the king.

"Wait a few days, sire, before deciding," said they upon returning to the castle. "A delay is better than a mistake."

While the king and his unpatriotic nobles delayed, Joan was compelled to be idle when her dear France sorely needed a leader. Orleans was besieged by the English, who had surrounded its walls by strong fortifications and closed all the gates save one. Orleans must be rescued before the Dauphin could go to Rheims to receive his crown.

Finally, even the Dauphin and his nobles could think of no reason for delaying longer. His Majesty appointed an evening for the interview, and Joan's thankfulness knew no bounds. To test the genuineness of her mission, the court took advantage of the maid's words and disguised the Dauphin. One of the nobles put on the king's royal garments and sat upon the throne beside the queen. The Dauphin, dressed as a gentleman of France, stood at some distance from the throne. When all was in readiness, one of the lords of the king's household was sent to conduct Joan to the great reception hall of the castle of Chinon.

Following her noble guide, heralded by the royal trumpeters, and attended by members of the royal household, she walked as quiet and as self-possessed as if among her forest trees at Domremy. The hall was lighted by a double row of torches held by bearers, and on either side stood princes and nobles with their ladies, all beautifully dressed and covered with jewels. It was a scene indeed to turn the head of any country maid.

Stopping a short distance from the throne, the nobleman bowed low, announced Joan's name, and stepped aside. Eager eyes watched to see what she would do. She neither bowed nor trembled. Looking straight into the eyes of the pretended king, she paused for a moment, troubled and uncertain, but not distressed. Then, as if convinced that she must look elsewhere for his Majesty, she quietly turned and scanned the faces on either side of the hall. Soon the look of uncertainty vanished from her face, and she hastened, smiling, to a gentleman standing a short distance from the throne. Kneeling and embracing his knees, she said in tones that touched the hearts of all hearers, "God give you long life, dear and gentle Dauphin!"

"Not so, my child," said the gentleman. "The Dauphin sits yonder, upon the throne."

"No, gracious Dauphin, I make no mistake," replied Joan.

"Then tell me who you are, and what you wish," replied the Dauphin, raising her from the floor.

"I am called Joan the Maid, and am sent of God with two messages to your Majesty. The King of Heaven wills that you shall be crowned king in your good city of Rheims. He also wills that you give me soldiers and set me to do my appointed work for France. For I am to raise the siege of Orleans and break the English power."

"These are brave words for a maid to speak," responded the king. "How shall I know that you are sent of God, and not an impostor?"

"You shall have proof that cannot be doubted, which I pray you let me whisper in your ear, for it is known only to you and to me." Then she drew him away from the others and whispered, "You fear that you are not the lawful heir to the throne. This fear takes away your hope and courage. It tempts you to abandon your kingdom and seek refuge in a foreign country. You are to doubt no more. You are the true and lawful heir of France. Hasten to use the means sent from heaven to secure your crown."

The young king raised his head and looked about him

with a new confidence and hopefulness. "No one knew of this anxiety except God and myself—I have never confessed it to a single soul. You could not have known it unless God revealed it to you. I am satisfied with the proof. I believe in your mission. Your petition is granted."

The king himself walked with Joan to the door and dismissed her with royal honors. She was no more delighted with these favors than she had been frightened by the unusual experience upon entering the great hall. Her heart was thankful for the promise of help. She was appointed commander in chief of the armies of France, with one of the royal princes as chief of staff. Soldiers, money, and provisions were easily obtained now that France had a leader once more. And at last, after many discouragements and much delay, Joan the Maid set out for the relief of Orleans.

Virtue Study

Work on Ephesians 6:10–11, the memory verse for this week.

1. Was Joan frightened when she entered the king's palace?
2. How did the king try to trick her?
3. Did Joan succeed in getting an army?

What do these verses say about how we should view rulers? Did Joan do these things?
- ♥ Proverbs 24:21
- ♥ Romans 13:1–7
- ♥ Titus 3:1
- ♥ Hebrews 13:17
- ♥ 1 Peter 2:17

WEEK 9 ~ DAY 3

The Valiant Maid of Orleans, Part 3
By Anna H. Carter, 1914

It was a wonderful sight, that great army. Joan rode at the head, with her standard bearer and her personal staff. A company of priests followed, the banner of the cross floating over them. After these came the different divisions of the army, commanded by the great generals of France.

Joan's army marched up the Loire to the relief of Orleans. Upon the river were a number of boats loaded with provisions which the people in the besieged city greatly needed. It was the business of the army to see that these boats arrived safely.

Joan planned to enter the city on the north side of the river, where the English were most strongly fortified. Before the army left Blois, the king had commanded that Joan's counsel should be obeyed without question. But the governor of Orleans and the generals of the army thought themselves wiser than this young country girl. They thought her plans too bold, and they secretly arranged to have the army march by the south bank.

When she arrived, she saw that the river lay between the army and the town and that the generals had not obeyed her. She was greatly distressed. When Dunois, the governor, came out to welcome her, she asked, "Are you Dunois, the governor of Orleans?"

"I am," said he, "and glad you have come to our aid."

"Did you give directions for the army to avoid the English by marching on this side of the river?"

"I, myself, and others wiser than I gave that advice. We thought the other plan too dangerous."

"The counsel of God is wiser and surer than yours. See the danger that confronts us. There, below the city, lie the boats of provisions. The wind is dead against them. Unless God sends help soon, they must fall into the hands of the enemy. You thought you deceived me, but you have deceived yourselves, for I bring a better rescue than ever came to soldier or city. I bring you the help of the King of Heaven."

Almost as she spoke the direction of the wind changed, the boats moved up to the city's one free gate, and the dangers from hunger were over. But the main part of the army was compelled to march back to Blois and return by the north side.

When all arrangements had been made for the march of the army, the maid, with one general and a thousand soldiers, went into Orleans with the governor. It was evening when she entered with her troops, riding a white horse and carrying her sword in her hand. Torches flamed, bells rang, and people crowded the streets to welcome the maid. There were rows upon rows of upturned faces, mouths wide open, shouting welcome, eyes overflowing with tears of joy and thanksgiving. The people kissed her feet, her sword, her bridle reins. She rode to the cathedral to give thanks, and the people followed her, adding their thanks to hers.

When the rest of the army arrived the next morning, Joan and her staff rode out to meet them. When the marching soldiers caught sight of the maid, they shouted for joy. When the march was finished, she returned to the front and rode at the head of the column, past the strongest fortification, and into the town. The English neither spoke nor fired a shot, although they stood in full view. The sight of the maid seemed to deprive them of the power of movement.

The next day, the first fortification was captured and destroyed, and the people's joy knew no bounds. On that day, they named her the Maid of Orleans, and her other titles were forgotten.

Being a wise general, and knowing that nothing increases courage like success, Joan urged her generals to follow up this victory by attacking the next fortification on the following day.

"We must be cautious and wait," urged the generals. "The English must be overcome by strategy. They are too numerous for our small army to oppose."

"We must be bold, and surprise them by moving quickly," replied Joan. "God is on our side, and He has promised us the victory." So in spite of schemes and delays, the battles continued, and every battle resulted in victory.

Once she was wounded by an arrow from a crossbow and fell from a scaling ladder to the ground. The English soldiers shouted for joy and hurried into the ditch to take her prisoner. The French soldiers rallied to the rescue, and the battle raged about her for a few minutes with the greatest fury.

The maid stood for France in the thoughts of both armies. Whichever won her would win France.

Finally she was rescued and carried away to have her wound dressed, and the battle went on without her. All day it raged, and toward nightfall, the French losing courage, the governor ordered the trumpeters to sound the retreat. Joan heard the bugles and understood. She countermanded the order. Mounting her horse, Joan rode to the place where she had been wounded. She ordered her standard bearer to let her standard blow free and to tell her when its fringes touched the wall. "It touches," said the bearer.

"Now," called Joan to the soldiers, "the place is yours! Buglers, sound the assault! Forward, brave hearts!"

Virtue Study

Work on Ephesians 6:10–11, the memory verse for this week.

1. How did Joan go into battle?
2. Why was it important for the soldiers to obey the orders of their leader?
3. Did Joan have good leadership skills?

Joan knew she would be involved in harsh battles, and so she wore a suit of armor. In Ephesians 6:10–20, Paul talked about how we should prepare ourselves for the spiritual battle that we are involved in every day. Read this passage and answer these questions.

- ♥ Why do we put on armor?
- ♥ Who do we fight?
- ♥ What makes up the armor?

WEEK 9 ~ DAY 4

The Valiant Maid of Orleans, Part 4
By Anna H. Carter, 1914

With a shout and a rush, the men filled the ditch and climbed up the ladders and over the fortifications. They met the enemy and fought, hand to hand, with the greatest fury. A fire boat set fire to the bridge, and when the English, driven out of the stronghold, tried to escape to a fort on the opposite side, they perished in the water. Following up this success, the last remaining fortress was attacked, and by sundown, Joan's banner floated from its walls. Victory was hers, and Orleans was rescued.

    She had done a great deed, and she received such homage as no other girl in all history has ever received. But Joan of Arc had a simple heart, and all this homage neither excited nor flattered her. Wounded and weary, she went to her quarters and fell asleep. The people stopped all traffic in the neighborhood and watched throughout the night to see that she slept undisturbed.

    Before dawn she was in the saddle and away on the road to Tours to report to the king. News of her victory went before her, and people flocked to see her pass. As in Orleans, they touched her hands, her feet, and her armor.

The king went to Tours to meet Joan. She knelt before him. The king removed his cap, stepped from the throne, and raised her to her feet.

"You must not kneel to me, my victorious general," said he. "You have gained a great victory and done a deed which my ministers and generals thought impossible, and the king should kneel to you. But you have been wounded, and the wound is still fresh. Sit here beside me. Now, before all these lords and ladies, tell me how I can reward you for this splendid service."

"Oh dear and gracious Dauphin, go with me to Rheims and be crowned. Do not lose a single day. The army is eager to gain more victories and will rejoice in clearing the way. Do not delay, I pray you, for the time is short."

"To Rheims? Impossible, my general. The road lies through the enemy's country. We must wait."

"Wait for what? If we wait, our soldiers will lose courage and desert the army, and the English will have time to strengthen their position."

"Still," insisted the king, "this is serious business, and I must first consult with my ministers. But you have not named your reward."

"I wish but one thing, and that is to go with you to Rheims, where all the kings of France are crowned," cried Joan, kneeling again.

"Was ever such unselfishness as this shown before?" asked the king, looking about him.

Drawing his sword, he touched Joan lightly on the shoulder. "Your proper place is among the nobles of France, to which I now join you. And for your sake, your family and relatives shall be ennobled. Rise, Joan of Arc, surnamed Du Lis in grateful acknowledgment of the victory you have won for the lilies upon the flag of France. You shall bear them, and the royal crown, and your own victorious sword upon your shield."

After many days of weary waiting, the king, Joan, and the army started for Rheims. They stopped on the way at Orleans, where they were received with great rejoicing. The entire city was in holiday array for their deliverer.

The English were first met at Jargeau, and were driven out after two days of hard fighting. Then, the maid with her army captured Meung, Beaugency, Patay, and Troyes. After that, the road to Rheims was free, and France was on the way to being free! The whole nation was wild with joy.

The march to Rheims began on a morning brilliant with sunshine and fresh with dew. The army was in fine condition and made a beautiful spectacle as it marched to the coronation. Joan, with the princes and their aides, took position for a last review of the army, for no one expected her ever to lead the army again. Her own purpose in going to Chinon in the first place had been to help crown the king. When that was done, she expected to return to her home in Domremy. Usually, in review, the soldiers cheered as they marched past the reviewing stand, drums beat, and bands played. Now, nothing could be heard but the tramp of thousands of marching feet. As the soldiers passed their general, they lifted hands in military salute and looked at her dear face in silent farewell.

Virtue Study

Work on Ephesians 6:10–11, the memory verse for this week.

1. How did Joan rescue Orleans?
2. From the very beginning, her mission was to help the Dauphin be crowned at Reims. Did she ever waver from this mission?
3. Why didn't she become conceited when the Dauphin showered praise and gifts on her?
4. What virtues did she display?
5. Does she remind you of anyone in the Bible? Look up Judges 4–5 for one example.

Read Judges 4–5 and answer these questions.
- ♥ Why did Deborah take the lead?
- ♥ Why didn't the men lead as they should have?
- ♥ Did Deborah try to take the power from Barak?
- ♥ How did Deborah view herself?

Box of Visual Reminders

Find a picture of a castle (look on the Internet or in a magazine). Put the picture in the box as a reminder of Joan's devotion. If you love to draw, create your own picture of a castle.

WEEK 9 ~ DAY 5

The Valiant Maid of Orleans, Part 5
By Anna H. Carter, 1914

When they arrived at the city, the walls were crowded with people and bright with flags bearing the lilies of France. Bands played, the streets were decorated, and every window along the way was bright with joyful faces.

The priests and mounted noblemen entered by the west door of the cathedral to the sound of solemn music and marched down the great central aisle to the altar front.

Hundreds of silver trumpets sounded, and Joan with the king appeared in the doorway, greeted by organ tones and clanging choirs and shouting people. Behind them marched the color bearer with Joan's white banner, followed the great lords of France. In the next group were the archbishop of Rheims and the bishops of three cities. Then came the generals who had led the armies of Joan of Arc.

The solemn ceremonies of the coronation began with songs and prayers and Scripture reading, Joan standing beside the king, the snowy banner in her hand. The king took the oath of loyalty to his country and was anointed with the sacred oil. A churchman, bearing the crown, knelt and offered it to the king. The king reached out his hands, hesitated, and looked at Joan. She nodded slightly, with a look of unspeakable joy and thankfulness. The king smiled, took the crown, and set it upon his head.

"Long live the king!" shouted the people. "Long live France!" Choirs chanted, the organ pealed, bells rang from all the steeples, Rheims went wild with joy. France at last had a king!

Joan, weeping and kneeling, said, "Now, gentle king, the will of God has been accomplished. My work is done. I pray you give me your blessing and let me return to Domremy. My father and mother are old and need my help."

The king, deeply moved, raised her and praised her there before the people who adored her.

"You have saved the crown, my wise and courageous general. Ask some favor of me. Whatever you ask shall be given you, though it take half my kingdom."

"Then, gracious king, I pray you excuse the village of Domremy from paying taxes. The people are poor and greatly distressed on account of the war, and they sorely need your help."

"It is so commanded," said the king. "What else?"

"Nothing, your Majesty."

"But you have asked nothing for yourself."

"I have no further blessing to ask, now that your Majesty is crowned."

The king in astonishment raised his head and spoke:

"This unselfish patriot has saved a kingdom, and all that she will accept from the king she has crowned is a favor for her native village. She has given all and requires nothing. Her patriotism is as great as her military skill and wisdom.

"It is well. I now declare that from this day forth, the village of Domremy shall be taxed no more. On the page of the tax book, where the name of Domremy and the amount of the taxes has heretofore been written, shall appear the words, "Nothing. The Maid."

This was all Joan would accept. For herself she desired nothing except to be allowed to go back to her village home to tend her sheep and be again with her mother. But Charles VII would not consent to that, for France was not yet free from the English.

So it was decided to try to recapture Paris. Shameful to say, however, the king did not give Joan the assistance he should, withdrawing instead from the city. Soon afterward, while leading an attack against the Duke of Burgundy, Joan was taken prisoner and sold to the English. King Charles made no effort to ransom her, nor did anyone else in France attempt to raise money to save her from her unhappy fate. She was charged with sorcery, put into prison, and after a year was brought to trial. At the trial she was found guilty, sentenced to death, and burned at the stake in the marketplace of Rouen, May 30, 1431.

A mere child in years, she rescued her country from the English by a series of brilliant victories, crowned the French king, and in return for this was burned alive at the stake, while those for whom she had fought looked on, making no effort to save her. She was seventeen years of age when she led the armies of France to victory, and but nineteen when she met her cruel death.

Her pure, steadfast, simple faith, together with her devotion to God and her patriotism, constitute her greatness. During her life in camp, in court, in her home, and in prison, she never forgot her womanly ideals, though she was called upon to do a man's work, and she stands today to all nations a shining example of pure and noble womanhood.

Virtue Study

Recite Ephesians 6:10–11, the memory verse for this week.

1. After all her glorious victories, what did Joan want to do?
2. What did she ask in return for her service?
3. Imagine that you lived in Joan's village long after she was dead. Instead of having to pay taxes each year, you were exempt. What would you think of Joan of Arc?

Joan saved her village from having to pay taxes. In a similar way, Jesus took away our sins. Just like a tax collector has a book with everyone's name and the money each owes, all of our sins are written down and held against us. Yet Jesus came and died for our sins. After we accept Jesus as our Lord and Savior, all those sins are removed. Only it's not with simple words like "Nothing. The Maid" written next to it—our sins are blotted out by the blood of Jesus.

What do these verses say about Christ's sacrifice?
- ♥ Hebrews 9:11–14
- ♥ 1 Peter 3:18
- ♥ 1 John 1:7–10
- ♥ 1 John 2:1–6

WEEK 10 ~ DAY 1

The Little Nurse, Part 1
By Rupert Sargent Holland, 1910

It was early summertime in England, just when the hawthorn dons its wonderful veil of pink and white along the roadsides, when the lilac bushes are bursting into purple blossom, and the soft turf beneath the stately oaks and beeches is thickly carpeted with daffodils.

This was a very beautiful part of English country, and a little girl named Florence loved it better each time she came back to it from her other home in the south. It was the rolling, romantic land of Derbyshire, right in the heart of England.

"Oh, but isn't it lovely, Max!" the girl exclaimed, looking down at an Ayrshire terrier. "Come along; we'll see what the garden's done."

Girl and dog raced around the house to the southern side. The gardens here sloped down in a series of wide terraces joined by stone steps. The girl stopped and drew a long breath of delight. Then she ran down the steps and bent above the flowers.

While she was busy looking at the flowers, two gentlemen came down the stone stairway that led from the library to the flagged terrace of Lea Hurst. "There's Florence," said one of the men to the other. "Give that little daughter of mine flowers or birds or animals of any sort to care for, and she's as happy as the day is long."

The other man, who was the vicar of the country church, smiled. "She ought to love such things. How could a girl with the lovely name of Florence Nightingale do otherwise?"

They walked down the steps of the garden. The girl, hearing their voices, sprang up and ran to meet them. "Oh, I'm so glad to see you again, Mr. Ritchie!" she cried. "We've missed you so much all winter."

"And we have missed you, little lady," said the vicar. "Mrs. Ritchie will be glad to know you're back in Derbyshire."

"Are you riding home now?" Florence turned impulsively to her father. "Please, sir, may I ride over with him to take tea with Mrs. Ritchie at the vicarage?"

"I'll see her safely home," said the clergyman.

Mr. Nightingale nodded. "Tell Sanders to saddle your pony and bring him with Mr. Ritchie's horse to the door. I wish I could go too, but I've letters to write."

The girl ran to the stables, and a little later she and the vicar were picking their way down the sloping drive of Lea Hurst to the valley. On and on they went, the vicar on his big horse; Florence, her brown hair flying in the wind, near him on her fleet-footed moorland pony.

The downs were dotted with grazing sheep, and finally the riders came to a place where they found a shepherd, an old bent man, trying to collect his scattered herd by hobbling after them and calling in cracked tones to them. He was working without success: the sheep only scattered farther.

The riders drew up and watched the old man's efforts. The vicar knew him. "Where's your dog, Roger?" he asked.

"The boys hereabouts have been throwing stones at him, sir," answered the shepherd, "and they've broken his leg, poor beast. He'll never be good for anything again, and I'm thinking of putting an end to his misery."

"You mean poor old Cap's leg is broken?" asked Florence. "Oh, can't we do something for him, Roger? It's cruel to leave him all alone in his pain. Where is he?"

"You can't do any good, missy," said the old shepherd sorrowfully. "I left him lying in the shed over yonder."

Florence looked pleadingly at Mr. Ritchie. "Oh, can't we do something for poor Cap?" she begged.

The vicar, seeing the pity in her face, turned his horse toward the distant shed, but Florence, with a word to her pony, dashed past him. She reached the shed first. Dismounting, she ran inside. In a corner lay the poor moaning sheepdog. Florence knelt down on the mud floor, and with the greatest care not to hurt him, touched his head with her soft hands and whispered soothing words to him until the dog lifted his big brown eyes and looked gratefully into her face.

The vicar had now come into the shed, and kneeling beside Florence, he examined the dog's leg. After a few minutes he said, "The stone only cut it. The bone is not broken. A little careful nursing ought to put him all right again."

"Oh, I'm so glad!" exclaimed Florence. "I love nursing. What should I do first?"

Virtue Study

Memory Verse: James 3:17. Write this verse on a 3 x 5 card and memorize it during the week.

1. What are some of the things that Florence loved?
2. What did she do when she heard of Cap's injury?
3. What does that show about her character?

She was obviously very compassionate. What do these verses say about compassion?
- ♥ Psalm 116:5
- ♥ Zechariah 7:9
- ♥ 2 Corinthians 1:3–4
- ♥ Ephesians 4:32

How did Jesus display compassion in these verses?
- ♥ Matthew 15:32
- ♥ Mark 1:41
- ♥ Mark 6:34

WEEK 10 ~ DAY 2

The Little Nurse, Part 2
By Rupert Sargent Holland, 1910

"Well," said the vicar, smiling at the girl's interest, "I should advise a hot compress put on Cap's leg."

"What's a compress?" asked Florence.

"It's a bandage made of cloths wrung out of boiling water and laid on the wound," explained Mr. Ritchie.

Delighted at the thought of helping the poor dog, the girl went out of the shed. Very near stood the shepherd's cottage, and lying on the grass in front of it was the shepherd's small boy. She went toward the cottage. "Is your mother at home?" she asked the boy. He shook his head. "She's gone to Derby town," he said. "Well, I want some boiling water," she explained. "Come help me." And without more ado, she went into the cottage kitchen.

The boy helped her light a fire, and they soon had the kettle boiling. Florence looked about for cloths for bandages, and she saw the old shepherd's clean smock hung up behind the door. "That's the very thing!" she exclaimed. "If I tear it up, Mamma'll give Roger another." So she took the smock and tore it into strips.

Then she told the boy to bring the kettle and a basin, and she went back to the shed.

With the help of the vicar, Florence soon had the hot bandages placed on Cap's swollen leg. She sat beside him, whispering to him, and calmed him so that he scarcely stirred when she changed the wrappings. At length Mr. Ritchie thought she ought to be going home. "Oh, no," begged Florence. "I want to see him get better. A nurse oughtn't to leave her patient. The boy can take my pony and ride over and tell them where I am."

The boy departed with his message, and the little nurse stayed with her charge, perfectly happy to be caring for him.

Shortly after sunset, old Roger came sorrowfully to the shed, thinking that his faithful friend would never be able to chase the sheep again. But as soon as he entered the shed, Cap greeted him with a whine of pleasure, turned his head toward him, and tried to get on his feet.

The shepherd was very much astonished. "Dear me, missy," said he, "why, you've been doing wonders! I never thought to see the poor dog greet me again."

"Yes, doesn't he look better?" said Florence. "Please help me make another compress."

"That I will, missy," agreed Roger heartily, and kneeling beside the girl and the dog, he fell to work with the strips of cloth and the hot water.

The vicar stood up. "Yes, Roger," said he. "Miss Florence is quite right. Your dog will be able to walk again if you give him a little rest and care."

The shepherd was quite overjoyed at the contented look in Cap's eyes and at the thought that he was not to lose him. "I'm sure I can't thank your reverence and the young lady enough," said he, "and you may be sure, sir, I'll carry out the instructions."

"I shall come again tomorrow, Roger," said Florence. "I know Mamma will let me when I tell her about Cap. I want to look after him until he's running about again."

"I hope you will, missy," answered the grateful shepherd. "I hope you will."

Florence gave the dog a final caress and whispered in his ear that she would come again. Then she and the vicar left the shed. The boy had come back with her pony, and she mounted and was soon flying back across the moors to Lea Hurst.

Virtue Study

Work on James 3:17, the memory verse for this week.

1. How did Florence help Cap?
2. How important was it to the shepherd to have his dog back?
3. What virtues did Florence have?

In our world today, we often place more importance on animals than we do on people. God gives us a clear perspective on how we should care for animals. What do these verses say about man and animals?
- ♥ Genesis 2:19–20
- ♥ Genesis 8:17
- ♥ Genesis 9:1–17
- ♥ Leviticus 24:21
- ♥ Psalm 8:4–8
- ♥ Proverbs 12:10

Box of Visual Reminders

Put a strip of white fabric in your box. Use this as a reminder of the bandages that Florence Nightingale made for Cap. We too need to be caring toward the sick.

WEEK 10 ~ DAY 3

Florence Nightingale and the Party
By Rupert Sargent Holland, 1910

There were two girls at the manor house, Florence and Frances, who were nearly the same age, and they studied and played together. They both loved flowers and animals, and each had her own garden and her own special pets. But Florence's heart was always touched by the poor beast or bird that had been hurt and had no one to care for it, and by the roadside wildflowers which had a hard time escaping cartwheels and the seedlings which had been blown to bare and rocky soil.

Mr. Nightingale soon saw that this daughter was a born gardener. When the day's lessons were over, she would pick up her little basket, which held a trowel, gardener's scissors, a water bottle, and a bundle of sharpened sticks, and hasten out-of-doors.

Sometimes he would follow her at a distance and watch her in the corner of a meadow digging up weeds that grew about the cowslips, or watering a little clump of daffodils that were trying to hold up their heads in the shade of a tree. Often she went far outside the gardens and meadows of Lea Hurst, where the hedges and the flowers were not so well cared for, and here she found plenty of work to do, propping up bruised plants, watering faded ones, and protecting others from careless cattle. Sometimes she found new flowers and transplanted some of them to her own garden at home; sometimes she found just the place where she thought lilies or marigolds ought to grow, and there she would plant and tend her charges so that another summer should find them blooming.

At home in the evenings, her father told her much about flowers and encouraged her to do all she could to search for old garden flowers which were growing scarce in Derbyshire and to cultivate them, to plant hardy blooms in waste places, to care for wildflowers, and to mend broken hedges. Besides her own formal garden on the terraced slopes of Lea Hurst, she soon had a dozen wild gardens scattered through the fields and half a hundred little flowerbeds which she visited regularly.

She loved the birds and the animals as much as her flowers. "Florence was born a nurse," said Mr. Nightingale to his wife. "I found her yesterday making a nest in a bush for a robin that had broken a wing. I dare say she intends to try to feed it."

So she did, whenever she found a bird that was hurt, a dog that was lame, or any creature that was suffering: she took the care of it to herself and invented ways by which it might be cured. The family called her "The Little Sister of Mercy," and her father gave her a place in one of the greenhouses for a hospital where she might look after her invalid birds and dogs.

The Squire, as Mr. Nightingale was called, took a great interest in the village that lay at the foot of the slope that was topped by Lea Hurst. With his wife and two daughters, he was continually planning picnics for the children and throwing open the gates of his beautiful manor to them and to all the neighbors. He loved to have them all share in his delight at the exquisite gardens, the perfect velvet lawns, the thick and well-kept hedges of yew and box, and the stalwart old shade trees that had been the glory of the place for many decades.

The great event of the summer was the children's "feast day," when all the boys and girls met at the schoolhouse and marched in a procession to Lea Hurst: the girls with big bouquets, or "posies," as they called them, in their hands; and the boys with sticks wound with flowers like small maypoles carried over their shoulders. The Squire always ordered a band, and this headed the merry march which swept out of the village and trudged up the hill to the great gates of the manor. There the children found tables waiting for them on the lawn, and they had only to camp there to be served with strawberries and cream and cakes and tea like real grownup guests. After this high tea, the band played and the children danced over the lawn and on the floor of a great tent Mr. Nightingale had set up in the garden.

The Squire's two daughters were continually inventing new games and leading in all the fun, and at the same time keeping a watchful eye for the smaller children who might tire easily. When the long summer twilight began to fade and the rich purple clouds to gather over the still valley of the Derwent, the band struck up a triumphal march and the children formed in line again and trooped up to the top terrace of the lawn. Here stood Mr. and Mrs. Nightingale to say good night, and as each guest went by, Florence or Frances gave them a present from a long table on the terrace.

Then each girl would bob a curtsey and each boy make a bow, and they all marched down the hill after the stirring band. So the "feast day" would come to a successful close, and the lord of the manor entertained his neighbors as was the good old English custom.

Virtue Study

Work on James 3:17, the memory verse for this week.

1. What did Florence do for fun?
2. How did she use her time?
3. What did the Nightingale family do for the children of the village?
4. What does it mean to be hospitable? Look this word up in a dictionary.

What do these verses say about being hospitable?
- Romans 12:13
- 1 Timothy 5:9–10
- 1 Peter 4:9–10
- 3 John 1:8

Florence loved to help things grow. Jesus tells a parable about the vine and branches in John. Read John 15:1–17 and discuss what it means to be connected to the true vine.

Box of Visual Reminders

Add a pleasant-smelling tea bag to your box. Let it remind you that we, as daughters of the King, are to practice hospitality just as Florence did.

Tea Party

For an additional activity, boil some water and have a tea party.

WEEK 10 ~ DAY 4

The Lady with the Lamp
By Rupert Sargent Holland, 1910

It did not take long for the people who lived near Lea Hurst in Derbyshire or in the neighborhood of Embley Park in Hampshire, where the Nightingales spent the autumns and winters, to appreciate "Miss Florence," as they called her. If anyone was sick or in trouble, there Miss Florence went, carrying flowers or fruit or a present of some sort with her, but always with the greater gifts of her happy smile, soft voice, and gentle, loving touch. The old people at the windows waved their hands to her as she drove down with her mother to church, and they smiled at the sight of the slender girl, dressed in a light summer muslin with a silk shawl across her back, her sweet face, with the soft brown hair smoothed down each side of it, beaming from the depths of a yellow Leghorn bonnet wreathed with roses.

The Squire's daughter Florence came to be a very angel to the poor of the Derwent valley. She would ride her pony over the heath to lonely cottages with a basket at her saddlebow filled with puddings and jellies, or carrying an armful of primroses and bluebells to some delicate woman or girl who longed for the wildflowers of the fields and hedgerows but could not go to them.

Everything about this girl was sunny. She had been born in the beautiful Italian city of Florence, the city of flowers, and had been named for it, and it seemed as though she had inherited that city's love of blossoms. Her gardens and the opportunities she had to nurse stricken pets were the chief joys of her childhood, and they were joys which grew as she grew up.

There were few good nurses in England in that day, and no schools where they could be taught. Florence Nightingale met a remarkable Quaker woman named Elizabeth Fry, who was trying to help women who were in prison. Together they visited many English hospitals and studied the methods of nursing. These methods were of the poorest, most useless sort.

At Kaiserswerth on the Rhine in Germany, a school for nurses had just been started, and there Florence Nightingale went to study. She learned a great deal and returned home to teach others. After a time, England went to war with Russia in the Crimea in Eastern Europe, and Miss Nightingale knew that many of the soldiers would lay down their lives there for want of proper nursing in the military hospitals. She felt that this was her call to service, and she offered to take a band of women nurses out to the Crimea to serve through the war.

Before the war had ended, Florence Nightingale had come to be as beloved by the British soldiers as the little girl of Lea Hurst had been by her father's neighbors. She was a wonderful nurse, because she was always full of courage and cheerfulness, never tiring, never shirking any labor that would ease suffering.

Thousands of wounded men watched for her to pass by their beds in the hospitals, and they declared they were better just for the sight of her face or the sound of her voice. She often took charge of men whose wounds the doctors had declared beyond curing and brought them back to health by her tireless care and patience.

After a time, she fell ill of cholera herself, and all England waited for news from her bedside. She recovered and was taken home. She went back to Lea Hurst and rested there while the whole country called her blessed. When the war was over, she returned to the London hospitals and continued the labors which were the great joy of her life.

The story of the work of this woman who tended the sick and the poor is one of the most beautiful in history. She asked nothing but the chance to serve, and thereby won the love of others.

Florence Nightingale Pledge

Mrs. Lystra Gretter wrote the Florence Nightingale Pledge in 1893. It was named after Miss Nightingale because of her contribution to the field of nursing:

"I solemnly pledge myself before God and in the presence of this assembly to pass my life in purity and to practice my profession faithfully. I will abstain from whatever is deleterious and mischievous, and will not take or knowingly administer any harmful drug. I will do all in my power to elevate the standard of my profession and will hold in confidence all personal matters committed to my keeping, and all family affairs coming to my knowledge in the practice of my calling. With loyalty will I endeavor to aid the physician in his work and devote myself to the welfare of those committed to my care."

Virtue Study

Work on James 3:17, the memory verse for this week.

1. What did Florence do when she grew up?
2. How did she serve her country?
3. What virtues did she have?

Florence was rich and had lots of servants, but instead of being spoiled by this, she decided to become a servant to others. What does God's Word say about being a servant?
- ♥ Matthew 20:25–28
- ♥ Luke 16:13
- ♥ John 12:26
- ♥ John 13:14–17
- ♥ Philippians 2:4–7

WEEK 10 ~ DAY 5

The Heroine of the Alamo
By Rufus C. Burleson, 1901

Susanna Dickenson and her husband, Lieutenant Dickenson, were born in Pennsylvania and brought up in Philadelphia, the "City of Brotherly Love." But when the cry came from Texas, struggling for freedom against the Mexicans, Lieutenant Dickenson said, "I must respond to freedom's call."

His young wife said, "I will go with you, my husband." He came, enlisted, and was made lieutenant in the immortal band of Captain William Barrett Travis, a young and dashing cavalier from Alabama.

On February 22, 1836, Santa Anna and his vanguard of five thousand veterans encamped around the Alamo and demanded an immediate and unconditional surrender. That insolent summons was answered with cannon shot and defiant shouts. Santa Anna immediately raised the blood-red flag of death. Then commenced that fearful siege of thirteen days and nights. During this time, Susanna displayed a courage that eclipsed the heroism of the Spartan mothers. For though her little daughter, Angelina, was only six weeks old, she cooked the food, prepared the bandages, washed and bound up the wounds, and by her words and heroic bearing cheered on the soldiers.

What mother on earth ever was called to listen alternately to the roar of the cannon, the groans of the dying, and the pitiful cry of her innocent babe? She saw the gashed bosom of her husband pouring out his lifeblood.

She caught his dying words, "God bless you, wife, I am dying. Take care of our babe."

On that fatal Sabbath morning, March 6, 1836, just as the church and convent bells were calling the devout to prayer, by the command of the angry Santa Anna his soldiers, with booming cannon, muskets, crowbars, and scaling ladders, rushed with brutal yells from all directions on the blackened walls of the Alamo.

The heroic band, worn out with thirteen days and nights of watching and fighting, with superhuman courage met and with deadly fire held back their assailants for the first and second time, but the common soldiers, goaded on by the shouts of their commanders and the spurs of the cavalry drawn up behind them, climbed up the scaling ladders while others battered down the doors and broke through the walls.

Susanna, with a mother's instinct, pressed her innocent babe to her bosom and silently gazed upon a scene of horror that no tongue or pen can ever describe. The holy place which had echoed with songs and praises for more than one hundred years now resounded with the deadly shot of guns and pistols, and the groans of the wounded and dying. Oh, what a scene for a mother and innocent babe to look upon!

At twelve o'clock on that beautiful Sabbath day, the bright sun looked down upon the dead bodies of the 182 heroes of the Alamo. At twilight's solemn hour, Susanna, with a woman's instinct, took her babe in her arms and a pitcher of water and visited the bleeding soldiers to see if any dying hero needed a cup of cold water or wished to send some message of love to mother or wife or sister far away. She found the dead bodies of Travis, Bonham, and Bowie. She found Crockett lying dead in a little confessional room in the northeast corner of the Alamo, with a huge pile of dead Mexicans lying around him.

Then the cruel Santa Anna sent Mrs. Dickenson, mounted on a mule with a baby in her arms, both sprinkled with blood, as a messenger of the defeat and bloody butchery of the Alamo. He hoped thereby to strike terror to all Texans. As she rode into the Texan encampment, hundreds of eager men gathered around her.

The first words she uttered were, "They all died fighting for liberty, as every true Texan should die."

As strong, rough men looked upon that mother and her little babe all sprinkled with blood, and heard her brave words, they sobbed aloud and cried "Revenge or death!" And "Remember the Alamo" became the battle cry.

Later in life, Mrs. Dickenson became a devoted Christian. She had been raised in the Episcopal Church, but she realized that she never knew anything about her lost condition or the true mission of the church till she heard a stirring sermon one night. The minister, Rufus C. Burleson, visited her at her home, and he wept and prayed with her. He found her a great bundle of untamed passions, devoted in her love and bitter in her hate. After many tears and prayers and religious instruction, she was joyfully converted. In less than two months, her change was so complete as to be observed by all her neighbors. At least fifteen hundred people crowded the banks of Buffalo Bayou one Sabbath evening to see her baptized. In the following years, she was a zealous laborer in every good work.

Virtue Study

Recite James 3:17, the memory verse for this week.

1. What important event did Susanna live through?
2. How did she respond to this situation?
3. What happened to her after the war?

God's Word tells us everything we need to know about how to live. Just because Susanna attended church didn't mean that she truly had a relationship with God. In the gospels and in Acts, there are several accounts of people who are converted. What do these verses say about how a person becomes a follower of Jesus Christ?
- ♥ John 3:1–21
- ♥ Acts 2:37–38
- ♥ Acts 9:1–19
- ♥ Acts 10:24–48

Have you ever made the decision to follow Christ? If you are ready to become a Christian, please follow the instructions that are outlined in the above verses.

WEEK 11 ~ DAY 1

The Lady Who Loved to Learn
By Charles Morris, 1904

The Duke of Northumberland persuaded Edward the Sixth of England to make a will saying who should reign after him. He would not name his half-sisters, Mary and Elizabeth. Instead, he named his cousin, Lady Jane Grey, who was only sixteen years old and was married to Lord Guildford Dudley, the son of the Duke of Northumberland. She and her husband were both Protestants, and the duke hoped that the people would rather have a Protestant queen than a Catholic like Mary. And then he thought that, as Lady Jane was his daughter-in-law, he would rule the country through her.

Lady Jane had been brought up very carefully. She was well educated. She knew Latin and Greek. She could speak French and Italian as well as her native tongue; she understood Hebrew, Chaldee, and Arabic; and she was able to play, sing, and do fancy embroidery. A very learned man named Roger Ascharn went to visit her parents in Broadgate, Leicestershire. He found all the family hunting deer in the park except this one young girl, Lady Jane, who instead sat reading a Greek book.

"I wonder that you like reading," said the visitor, "better than hunting deer."

She answered, "All their sport in the park is but a shadow of the pleasure that I find in my book. Alas, good folks, they never knew what good pleasure meant."

"And how came you," asked Roger Ascham, "to this deep knowledge of pleasure, and what did chiefly allure you to it, seeing that not many men and very few women attain thereto?"

She answered, "Sir, God hath blessed me with sharp and severe parents and a gentle schoolmaster. For when I am in the presence of either father or mother, whether I speak, keep silence, sit, stand, or go, eat, drink, be merry or sad, be singing or dancing, or at anything else, I must do it, as it were, in such weight, measure, and number, even as perfectly as the world was made; or else I am so sharply taunted and cruelly threatened, yea, presently sometimes with pinches, and so cruelly disordered, that I think myself in hell till the time come that I go to Mr. Aylmer, who teacheth me so gently, so pleasantly, with so fair allurements to learning, that I think all the time is as nothing while I am with him. Thus my book hath been so much more pleasure, and bringeth daily to me more pleasure, and more that, in respect of it, all other pleasures in very deed be but trifles and very troubles with me."

She did not care for rich dresses and would have been content to live a quiet country life with her pretty garden and her many books rather than to have been queen of England.

As soon as Edward the Sixth was dead, her father and mother and her husband's father and mother came to see her. They told her of her cousin's death and explained to her that she must be queen, and they gave their reasons. Then her husband and his father, and some other lords who were present, fell on their knees and did homage to her as queen.

The poor child was horrified at the news of her cousin's death. When she heard that she was to be queen of England, which was the last thing she wanted to be, she screamed aloud and fainted away. When she came to herself again, she begged that they would not try to make her queen, but would leave her to be happy in her own way.

"I will not be queen," she said, but her father and mother insisted that she must be, and they threatened her with all sorts of punishments if she refused, and her husband and his parents persuaded her.

"Don't hold back," they said, "and endanger the Protestant cause by faintheartedness."

She yielded at last, and, as she afterwards wrote to Mary, "I turned myself to God, humbly praying and entreating Him that, if this which was given me were rightly and lawfully mine, His Divine Majesty would give me such grace and spirit that I might govern to His glory and the welfare of this realm."

When she had recovered from the shock and had been arrayed for the occasion, Jane was taken by water to the Tower. She entered it in state, her train being borne by her mother, and at her entrance the Lord Treasurer presented her with the crown, while her relations saluted her on their knees.

The same evening, heralds proclaimed round London that Edward was dead and that Jane was queen, but the Londoners were not pleased, for they wanted Mary or Elizabeth to be queen. The people of London looked on Lady Jane Grey as a usurper, and though Northumberland and Lady Jane's father got together an army, it was in vain, for Queen Mary was proclaimed from Paul's Cross amid shouts of joy from all the people. There were bonfires and sounds of joy, whereas, when Lady Jane was proclaimed queen, there had only been a miserable silence.

Virtue Study

Memory Verse: Philippians 4:13. Write this verse on a 3 x 5 card and memorize it during the week.

1. What kind of parents did Jane have?
2. What kind of teacher did she have?
3. Why did she love to spend time learning?

What does this verse say about students and teachers?
- Luke 6:40

What do these verses say about paying attention to the teaching you receive?
- Exodus 33:13
- Deuteronomy 11:19–21
- Psalm 25:4–5
- Psalm 51:6
- Proverbs 6:20–22
- Proverbs 7:2
- 2 Thessalonians 2:15

WEEK 11 ~ DAY 2

The Nine Days' Queen, Part 1
By Charles Morris, 1904

Just nine days after they had made her queen, Jane was taken back to her own house. Her whole time during her brief reign had been made miserable by her husband and his mother, because though she would make him a duke, she had made up her mind that she would not let him call himself king. He scolded and tormented her, and then sulked and would not speak to her, so that she was very miserable and tired of playing at being queen. She was glad to go back to being only Lady Jane Grey.

The Duke of Northumberland saw that his plans had failed, so he tried to save himself by pretending to be very glad that Queen Mary had ascended to the throne.

"The queen is merciful," he said, "she will pardon me."

"Don't think of it," answered a gentleman who was with him. "Whoever else escapes, you will not."

The Princess Mary was at this time far from London. The crafty Duke of Northumberland had at first tried to keep the death of young King Edward a secret until he could get the two princesses into his power. But the Earl of Arundel, who knew of it, and was a friend of Princess Mary, secretly sent word to her that her brother was dead and that Lady Jane Grey had been named as queen in his will. Mary was then riding to London to see her sick brother, but on hearing of his death and her own danger, she turned the head of her horse and rode at full speed into the county of Norfolk.

Here some powerful lords declared that Mary was the true queen and raised troops to support her cause. They had her proclaimed queen at Norwich and gathered around her at the Castle of Framlingham, which belonged to the Duke of Norfolk. She was not safe, and it was thought best to keep her in a castle on the seacoast, where she might be sent abroad if necessary.

When news of this came to London, the council of the kingdom, which felt that it must obey the king's will, wished to send Lady Jane's father, the Duke of Suffolk, as the general of the army, against this force. But she implored that her father might remain with her. He was known as a weak man, and they told the Duke of Northumberland that he must take the command himself.

He was not ready to do so, as he mistrusted the council, but there was no help for it. He set forth with a heavy heart, observing to a lord who rode beside him at the head of the troops that, although the people pressed in great numbers to look at them, they were terribly silent.

His fears for himself turned out to be well-founded. While he was waiting at Cambridge for further help from the council, they took it into their heads to turn their backs on Lady Jane's cause and to take up the Princess Mary's. This was chiefly owing to the Earl of Arundel, who said to the mayor and town leaders in an interview with them that, as for himself, he did not perceive the reformed religion to be in much danger if Mary were to become queen.

Thus the mayor and leaders changed their minds very quickly, and said there could be no doubt that the Princess Mary ought to be queen. So she was proclaimed, at the Cross by St. Paul's.

It was now plain that Lady Jane's reign was at an end. She very willingly gave up the crown, saying that she had accepted only in obedience to her father and mother, and went gladly enough back to her pleasant house by the river and to her books, which she loved far more than she did power.

Mary, at this time, was coming toward London. At Wanstead, in Essex, she was joined by her half-sister, the Princess Elizabeth. They passed through the streets of London to the Tower, and there the new queen met some important prisoners then confined in it, kissed them and gave them their liberty.

Virtue Study

Work on Philippians 4:13, the memory verse for this week.

1. Why did Jane's father-in-law want her to be queen?
2. What happened to Jane when the people turned against her?
3. Did Jane want to be queen?

Many times in history, innocent people have been pushed forward by selfish people who want to use them for their own gain. Lady Jane Grey was one of those people. Was her head turned by the crown they gave her?

What do these verses say about what kind of crown we should strive for?
- Proverbs 12:4
- Isaiah 51:11
- Isaiah 61:3
- Isaiah 62:3
- 1 Corinthians 9:25
- 2 Timothy 4:8
- James 1:12
- 1 Peter 5:4

What items make up the crowns mentioned in these verses?
- Proverbs 10:6
- 1 Thessalonians 2:19

WEEK 11 ~ DAY 3

The Nine Days' Queen, Part 2
By Charles Morris, 1904

The Duke of Northumberland was imprisoned, and together with his son, Lady Jane's husband, and five others, was quickly brought before the council. He asked that council whether it was treason to obey orders that had been issued by the king, but the council still found him guilty. When he ascended the scaffold to be beheaded on Tower Hill, he addressed the people in a miserable way, saying that he had been incited by others and exhorting them to return to the Catholic religion, which he told them was his faith. Perhaps he expected Queen Mary to pardon him for his confession, but she did not, and he was executed.

As for Lady Jane, she was not allowed to stay long in her pleasant room among her books, but was taken from there and shut up in the Tower of London along with her husband. They were permitted to walk about in the gardens of the Tower, but they were prisoners. To be sure Lord Dudley, her husband, no longer tormented her with his petty desire to be called king. He could not now even bear the title of duke, which she had promised him. There were those who wished Queen Mary to have her girlish rival's head cut off, as had long been the fashion in such cases, but the new queen would not consent.

"I am not afraid of Jane Grey," she said. "She has no friends powerful enough to do me any harm, and why should I take the life of that insignificant girl, who will never be anything but a mere bookworm?"

Soon after Mary was crowned Queen of England at Westminster, her sister Elizabeth, who would follow her on the throne if she should die without children, carried the crown of England from the Abbey Church to Westminster Hall on a cushion. She complained to the French ambassador that the crown was very heavy.

"You will not find it so," he said, "when you are queen and you have to wear it on your own head."

Queen Mary wanted to marry a Spanish prince, he who afterwards became the cruel Philip II, but the English people hated the Spaniards—partly on account of their brutality, partly because they were Roman Catholics. A gentleman named Sir Thomas Wyatt, with several other nobles, made a plot to take the crown from Mary and make Princess Elizabeth queen.

Lady Jane Grey's relations had taken advantage of the disturbances to proclaim publicly that she ought to be queen, and Queen Mary was so angry at this, that, although Lady Grey knew nothing about it, Mary did one of the cruelest acts of her bloody reign. She sentenced poor Lady Jane and her husband to be executed.

Lady Jane received the news of her sentence very bravely and quietly. She wrote a letter to her father on the blank leaves of a Greek Testament, and another letter to her sister Catherine. This was written in Greek, to prevent its being read by the guards who surrounded her.

They offered to let her see her husband again for the last time before her head and his were taken off, but she refused, saying that she had need of all her courage, and she might break down if she saw him. She seems to have been fond of him, though he was so disagreeable to her when she would not agree to let him be called king.

Early in the morning, poor Lady Jane Grey stood by the iron-barred window of her prison and saw her poor young husband led out to be beheaded. About an hour later, as she still stood by the window in prayer, she saw a common cart come through the gate, and in it her husband's body, all covered with blood. She wrote in Latin, "Man's justice destroyed his body, God's mercy preserves his soul." And in English she wrote, "If my fault deserved punishment, my youth and imprudence were worthy of excuse." The governor of the Tower asked her for a keepsake when he came to lead her to the scaffold, and she gave him a little book.

She came up to the scaffold with a firm step and a quiet face, and addressed the bystanders in a steady voice. They were not numerous, for she was too young, too innocent, and too fair to be murdered before the people on Tower Hill, as her husband had just been. The place of her execution was within the Tower itself.

She said she had done an unlawful act in taking what was Queen Mary's right, but that she had done so with no bad intent, and that she died a humble Christian. Her last words reflected her faith as she said, "Lord, into Thy hands I commend my spirit." Lady Jane Grey died bravely, and she is remembered for her humility and faith.

Virtue Study

Work on Philippians 4:13, the memory verse for this week.

1. How did Jane suffer for the actions of her parents and in-laws?
2. Why did Queen Mary have Jane beheaded?
3. What virtues did Jane have?

Jane knew where she was going when she died. How should a Christian view death? What do these verses say about that?
- Psalm 116:15
- Ecclesiastes 5:15
- John 5:24
- John 11:25–26

It is natural for humans to fear death, but Jesus conquered the grave, and as His daughters, we should not fear death. What do these passages say about that?
- Acts 2:22–24
- Romans 6:8–10
- Romans 8:38–39
- 1 Corinthians 15:54–55

Box of Visual Reminders

Jane Grey loved to learn because she had a kind teacher. Place a pen in your box to remind you that learning is valuable. The most important thing we can learn is the truth found in God's Word.

WEEK 11 ~ DAY 4

Battling for the Boys in Blue, Part 1
By Louis Banks, Margaret Davis, and Julia Chase

Mary A. Bickerdyke was universally known as Mother Bickerdyke. Her marvelous work for the wounded Northern soldiers was a labor of love, and her heroism was born of self-sacrificing devotion that knew no limit. When the Civil War broke out, she was a middle-aged widow living in Illinois. The horrific conditions in field hospitals led her to volunteer as a nurse. From the beginning, she worked tirelessly for the boys in blue.

After the battle of Shiloh, Mother Bickerdyke was found by one of the surgeons wrapped in the gray overcoat of a Confederate officer, for she had disposed of her shawl to some poor fellow who needed it. She was wearing a soft slouch hat, having lost her usual bonnet. Her kettles had been set up, the fire kindled underneath, and she was dispensing hot soup, tea, crackers, and other refreshments to the shivering, fainting, and wounded men.

"Where did you get these articles?" the surgeon inquired, "and under whose authority are you at work?"

She paid no heed to his questions, and probably did not hear them, so completely absorbed was she in her work of mercy.

Watching her with admiration for her skill, administrative ability, and intelligence—for she not only fed the wounded men, but dressed their wounds in many cases—the doctor approached her again. "Madam, you seem to combine in yourself a sick-diet kitchen and a medical staff. May I inquire under whose authority you are working?"

Without pausing in her work, she blurted out, "I have received my authority from the Lord God Almighty. Have you anything that ranks higher than that?" As a matter of fact, she held no position whatever at that time. She was only a volunteer nurse and had not yet received an appointment, but her answer revealed the real spirit and purpose of the noble woman.

Mother Bickerdyke was always helpful in an emergency. While stationed at Memphis, she found that the people in the enemy's country were charging enormous prices for milk and eggs, and that the most useless produce was being sent to the hospital. One day she exclaimed to the doctor, "Do you know we are paying fifty cents for every quart of milk we use? And do you know it is such poor stuff—two-thirds chalk and water—that if you should pour it into the trough of a respectable pig at home, he would turn up his nose and run off, squealing in disgust?"

"Well, what can we do about it?" asked the doctor.

"If you'll give me thirty days' furlough and transportation, I'll go home and get all the milk and eggs that the Memphis hospitals can use."

"Get milk and eggs! Why, you could not bring them down here if the North would give you all it has. A barrel of eggs would spoil in this warm weather before it could reach us, and how on earth could you bring milk?"

"But I'll bring down the milk and egg producers. I'll get cows and hens, and we'll have milk and eggs of our own. The folks at home, Doctor, will give us all the hens and cows we need for the use of these hospitals, and jump at the chance to do it. You needn't laugh or shake your head!" she said as he turned away, amused and skeptical. "I tell you the people in the North ache to do something for the boys down here, and I can get fifty cows in Illinois alone, for just the asking."

"Pshaw! Pshaw!" said the doctor, "you would be laughed at from one end of the country to the other if you should go on so wild an errand."

"Fiddlesticks! Who cares for that? Give me a furlough and transportation, and let me try it."

When Mother Bickerdyke was in that mood there was no stopping her, and North she went. She was escorted as far as St. Louis by several hundred cripples, every one of whom had lost either a leg or an arm. These she saw placed in hospitals, and then went to Chicago. Jacob Strawn, a big hearted farmer, with a few of his neighbors, gave her a hundred cows at once.

Before her thirty days' leave of absence was ended, Mother Bickerdyke returned to Memphis in triumph, amidst the lowing of a hundred cows and the cackling of a thousand hens. Former slaves were detailed to take charge of them, and after that there was an abundance of fresh milk and eggs for the use of the hospitals.

Virtue Study

Work on Philippians 4:13, the memory verse for this week.

1. What did Mother Bickerdyke do for her country?
2. In what ways did she serve the soldiers?
3. Who did she look to as her authority?
4. What virtues did she have?

What do these verses say about diligence?
- Proverbs 12:24
- Proverbs 13:4
- Proverbs 21:5
- 1 Timothy 4:15
- Hebrews 6:10–12

In Matthew, Jesus tells a parable about ten virgins. Five of them were prepared, and five were foolish. Mother Bickerdyke was certainly prepared for emergencies. Read Matthew 25:1–13 and answer these questions:
- What did the wise virgins do?
- What did the foolish virgins ask of the wise ones?
- What happened to the foolish virgins?

WEEK 11 ~ DAY 5

Battling for the Boys in Blue, Part 2
By Louis Banks, Margaret Davis, and Julia Chase

During the siege of Vicksburg, an officer who had charge of the hospital supplies was discovered by Mother Bickerdyke in the act of using them dishonestly. She would not permit such actions. That he should be interfered with by her was more than his dignity could tolerate, and with all the ceremony of offended authority, he complained to General Sherman.

"Who is she?" inquired the general.

"A Mother Bickerdyke," he scornfully replied.

"Oh! Well," said the general, "she outranks me; you must apply to President Lincoln."

The disconcerted officer slunk quickly away while the general indulged in a smile of amusement. Mrs. Bickerdyke was well known to him. He appreciated her remarkable abilities and secured her services for his men when the autumn campaign began.

After the battle at Chattanooga, Mother Bickerdyke found herself face to face with the bitterest enemy of all—winter. On New Year's Day in 1864, when all the elements seemed combined to create a reign of terror, it was discovered by two o'clock in the afternoon that the fuel was giving out. To send men out into the forest to cut more in the awful coldness seemed barbarous. The surgeon in charge dared not order them out, and it is doubtful if the order could have been obeyed had it been given.

"We must try to pull through until another day," he said, "for nothing can be done tonight." And he retired to his own quarters in helplessness.

Mrs. Bickerdyke was equal to the emergency. With her usual disdain of red tape, she appealed to the Pioneer Corps to take their mules, axes, hooks, and chains, and tear down the breastworks near them, which were made of logs with earth thrown up against them. They were of no value, having served their purpose during the campaign. Nevertheless, an order for their demolition was necessary if they were to be destroyed.

There was no officer of sufficiently high rank present to dare give this order, but after she had refreshed the shivering men with a hot drink, they went to work at her suggestion, without orders from officers. The lives of the wounded men would be in danger if the fires went out. The men of the corps set to work tearing down the breastworks and hauling the logs to the fierce fires while Mrs.

Bickerdyke ordered half a dozen barrels of meal to be broken open and mixed with warm water for their mules.

In the morning, the officer in command of the post was informed of Mrs. Bickerdyke's unauthorized actions. He hastened down to where the demolished breastworks were being rapidly devoured by the fierce flames. He took in the situation immediately and evidently saw the necessity and wisdom of the course she had pursued, but it was his business to preserve order and maintain discipline, and so he made a show of stopping the irregular proceeding.

"Madam, consider yourself under arrest!" was the major's address to the busy Mrs. Bickerdyke.

To which she replied, as she flew past him with hot bricks and hot drinks, "All right, Major, I'm arrested, only don't meddle with me till the weather moderates, for my men will freeze to death if you do." A story got in circulation that she was put in the guardhouse by the major, but this was not true.

There was some little official hubbub over her night's exploits, but she defended herself to the officers who reproved her with this indisputable statement, "It's lucky for you that I did what I did, for if I hadn't, hundreds of men in the hospital tents would have frozen to death. No one in the North would have blamed me, but there would have been such a hullabaloo about your heads for allowing it to happen that you would have lost them whether or no."

Some of the officers stood boldly by her, openly declaring that she had done right, and advised her to pursue the same course again under the same circumstances. This was heedless advice, as she would assuredly have done so.

Virtue Study

Recite Philippians 4:13, the memory verse for this week.

1. How did her character give her credibility with the generals?
2. What did she do when faced with freezing weather?
3. Sometimes it's important to be creative and find ways around challenging difficulties. Was it more important to save lives or to preserve the breastworks that were no longer being used?
4. What virtues did Mother Bickerdyke display?

Mother Bickerdyke was a woman of integrity, and that kept her out of trouble when she didn't follow military guidelines. What do these verses say about integrity?

- ♥ Psalm 25:21
- ♥ Proverbs 10:9
- ♥ Proverbs 11:3
- ♥ Proverbs 13:6
- ♥ 1 Chronicles 29:17

Mother Bickerdyke saw a lot of things during her life. Read Ecclesiastes 3:1–8. What do these verses say about there being a time for everything?

Box of Visual Reminders

Mother Bickerdyke saved many lives by keeping the fires going on a cold winter night. Place a small piece of wood in your box to remind you of her quick thinking in an emergency.

WEEK 12 ~ DAY 1

Upheaval in China, Part 1
By Katharine S. Cronk and Elsie Singmaster, 1921

It was New Year's Eve in China, even though the calendar on Jennie Crawford's desk in the hospital in the city of Hanyang said "January 31, 1911." Three years ago, she had left her home in Lynn, Massachusetts, to go to Hanyang because there were more nurses in the state of Massachusetts than in all the great Chinese Empire.

"If I should live in China fifty years," she said to herself as she looked at her calendar, "I'll never get used to February 1st or any other day than the first day of January being New Year's Day. It seems so strange to have a different day every year and none of them January 1st."

She walked to the window and looked out. The night was stormy. Loud peals of thunder startled the people who hurried along the streets, and occasional flashes of lightning illuminated the crowds gathered there.

"It's not a good sign for the New Year," said one old Chinese to another. "When it thunders on New Year's Eve, it will be a bad year!"

"We must make sure tonight that the evil spirits are all frightened away," answered his friend. "We must take no chances of any being left to get into the New Year."

The two men joined the crowd, who were beating gongs and setting off firecrackers. Here and there, Buddhist priests went up and down, urging the people to make just as much noise as possible.

Inside the houses, mothers were trying to rouse their sleepy children, because unless the whole family kept awake and very watchful, the evil spirits would get into the houses and stay all the year. When the sleepy children could no longer hold their tired eyes open, their mothers hurriedly fed them a vegetable with a bad odor so that the spirits might be frightened away.

New Year's Day was clear and beautiful, and all China had a holiday. The shops were closed, and the houses were decorated with strips of red paper inscribed with Chinese characters which meant "happiness," "long life," and other blessings. On most of the doors were pasted new pictures of idols. These were the "door gods" who were expected to frighten the evil spirits away.

It was a busy morning for Jennie Crawford. As in most hospitals, there seemed to be more work than there were people to do it. She assisted with two operations; she made a visit to every bed, sometimes saying only a word of encouragement, but more often lending a hand in a delicate dressing or superintending the bathing of a very ill patient. She was an expert nurse, and the poor women and children looked at her affectionately, knowing that when her tender hands were compelled to hurt them, it was because she loved them.

As Miss Crawford looked down the street, she could tell the houses of Christians because on them were no hideous pictures, but instead, beautiful verses from the Bible giving God's promise to care for those who trust in Him.

Everyone goes calling on New Year's Day in China, and many callers came to bring good wishes to Miss Crawford. Little Mrs. Tsao, the wife of the Chinese Christian pastor, came early. Her hair was brushed until it shone like folds of black satin.

"Oh, that the light of God may this year shine upon China just as the sun shines today!" she said.

Next came Miss Crawford's Chinese teacher, who was so dressed up for the New Year that she scarcely knew him. He did not lift his hat as he came in, for that would have been most impolite. From the long, full sleeve of his coat, he took a package wrapped in a yellow silk handkerchief. He unwrapped the package and handed one of his large, red paper calling cards to Miss Crawford.

A procession of fifteen men from the Christian church came together. Each man bowed very low and shook his own hand instead of Miss Crawford's to wish her a happy New Year.

All day long, the callers came and drank tea and ate Chinese sweets. In the evening, Miss Crawford and her friend, Jennie Cody, a teacher in the Bible school, sat down together.

"The people in Hanyang are learning to trust us and to really love us," said Jennie Crawford happily. "Better still, they are learning to trust and love God. Did you notice how many of the doors had Bible verses over them today instead of those hideous gods? I'm glad every day that I came to China."

Virtue Study

Memory Verse: 1 Timothy 4:12. Write this verse on a 3 x 5 card and memorize it during the week.

1. Why did Miss Crawford go to China?
2. What kind of work was she doing?

It was easy for Miss Crawford to know who was a Christian and who was not simply by what they hung over their door on New Year's Day. In our culture, it's not always as easy to know if a person is a follower of Christ. What are some ways that Christians in our day try to let people know they worship Christ?

In the Old Testament, God told the people of Israel how to remember the words of the Lord. Read Deuteronomy 11:18–21.
- ♥ How should a family actively remind themselves of God's words?

Read John 13:35.
- ♥ What is the sign of a disciple?

In Acts there is a story of a woman named Dorcas. Jennie Crawford was like Dorcas in that they both helped others. Read Acts 9:36–41 and answer these questions:
- ♥ What kind things did Dorcas do?
- ♥ What happened to her?
- ♥ What miracle did Peter do for her?

WEEK 12 ~ DAY 2

Upheaval in China, Part 2
By Katharine S. Cronk and Elsie Singmaster, 1921

"Would you still be glad if we had such fighting and riots here as they had across the river in Hankow last week?" asked Jennie Cody.

Jennie Crawford laughed. "I've never had a chance to find out what I would do in a battle," she said.

"Things look as if you might have a chance to find out very soon," said Jennie Cody.

Presently, a native Bible teacher came in and sat down with them.

"We were talking about the rumors of war," said Miss Crawford. "Do you think there will really be a revolution?"

"There must be a revolution," she answered. "You Americans would never have had freedom to govern your own country if you had not had your revolution. It is even worse in China. Three hundred years ago, the Manchus came from the north and took the government away from the Chinese, put a Manchu emperor on the throne, and made the yellow flag with its dragon the flag of China. They compelled the men of China to fix their hair in queues, which was a braided ponytail near the nape of the neck. Whenever a Chinese man dared to cut off his queue, the soldiers of the emperor cut off his head. The Chinese want to be free to rule their own land as you do in America."

"I wish that China was a republic like the United States, but I'm afraid I'd make a poor soldier in a revolution," said Jennie Cody.

In October came rumors of riots and warfare. One evening as Jennie Crawford sat writing in her room, she heard a loud knocking at the door and a voice calling. There stood Jennie Cody, holding up a letter. She had sped across the drill ground of the school and along the dark city wall to the hospital.

"A letter has come from the father of a pupil," she gasped. "He is a Chinese official, and he says there are rumors that a rebellion will start tomorrow."

"We have heard many rumors of war," said Jennie Crawford. "This is only another."

The next day passed, and the next and the next, and still nothing happened. That night she slept without fear.

Early the following morning, a Christian woman came to her. "I've been up all night," she said. "The people are fleeing to the country by hundreds, carrying on their backs bundles of bedding and clothing. All night there has been a procession leaving the city. They say the revolution is beginning and that the hardest fighting will be in Hanyang because the guns and powder are stored here in the great arsenal. Both armies will try to capture that."

Before noon another letter came. Jennie Crawford read it quickly.

"The American consul says, 'All American women and children must leave Hanyang for a place of safety at once. Fighting has begun nearby!'"

Dr. Huntley, the physician in charge of the hospital, called a meeting of all the missionaries.

"We don't want to go," said Jennie Crawford. "The school is full of girls, and the hospital is full of patients. We don't want to leave them."

It was agreed that the women and children in the hospital and the girls in the school would be safer at their homes. Jennie Crawford and the teachers found escorts for pupils and patients, while Dr. Huntley went across the river to Hankow to talk to the British consul.

"The missionaries in Wuchang thought they would not have to leave," said the consul. "Now the gates of the city have been closed. The American consul has been trying to get them out, but he cannot reach them. Fighting is going on all round the mission. You must get the American women and children out of Hanyang before the soldiers enter."

Dr. Huntley hurried home. The frightened boatman did not want to wait a minute. As he stepped out of the boat, Dr. Huntley took out his watch.

"It is twenty minutes after four," he said. "Promise me that you will wait here with your boat until five."

The boatman promised, and the doctor hurried to the hospital. At the tea table in the dining room sat Mrs. Huntley with Jennie Crawford and Jennie Cody.

"We have no choice; we must leave in thirty minutes," announced Dr. Huntley. "Get together a few things and take no more than you can carry."

The half-emptied teacups left on the table as the women hurried from the dining room were to remain there many days. Gathering up a few things, they started for the boat as the sun was setting. On a hill behind the hospital were six hundred soldiers of the Manchu Emperor.

"They are likely to fire!" said one of the servants.

But no gun was fired as the party went out. The boatman was waiting, although he trembled with fear. The river was rough, and the waves threatened to swallow the little boat, but it reached Hankow in safety.

Virtue Study

Work on 1 Timothy 4:12, the memory verse for this week.

1. What did Miss Crawford do when she heard rumors of war?
2. Why did she want to stay at her post?
3. What does this tell us about her character?
4. Do you think Miss Crawford counted the cost of following Christ when she became a missionary nurse? Why or why not?

Sometimes following God is not easy, and just because someone is a missionary doesn't mean that he or she will be protected from all harm. Read 2 Corinthians 11:23–33. What type of troubles did Paul go through during his work as a missionary?

Miss Crawford went to China because she wanted to share God's love. Read 1 Corinthians 13. How does God define love?

WEEK 12 ~ DAY 3

Upheaval in China, Part 3
By Katharine S. Cronk and Elsie Singmaster, 1921

The city was crowded, and the only rooms to be found were in a poor little hotel. None of the party slept that night.

"If you hear a signal in the night," they were warned, "it will mean, 'Danger! Rise and dress!' If there is a second signal, it will mean, 'All gather near the gunboats!' A third signal will mean, 'Great danger! American women and children get into the boats!'"

All night they listened, but they heard only the steady tramp, tramp, tramp of the guards who marched up and down the streets.

In the morning, a messenger called out, "The soldiers entered Hanyang in the night!"

If the boatman had not waited, they would have been shut up in the city!

"Rich Chinese men and women are paying lots of money to be let down over the walls in baskets, for the gates are closed, and no one can get out any other way," said the messenger.

In the evening, Jennie Crawford saw thirty girls coming down the street.

"Here come the schoolgirls from Wuchang!" she cried joyfully.

Each girl carried the few clothes she had been able to save tied up in a square cotton cloth.

"For two days and nights, we were shut in the school building," said one. "The bullets flew all around, and we could see burning buildings every way we looked. Then the rescue party reached us. We had our bundles all ready to leave at a moment's notice."

They were very tired, yet they stood bravely round the walls of the room, for there were no chairs. Not one knew whether she had a home or any friends left, but not even the youngest cried or complained.

"Extra! Extra!" shouted a newspaper messenger as he carried his papers from house to house. "Twenty thousand troops on the way from Peking!"

Jennie Crawford bought a paper, and everyone gathered round her.

"Twenty thousand of the emperor's soldiers are on their way from Peking!" she announced. "The British and American consuls advise all foreign women and children to go on to Shanghai!"

On to Shanghai they went that evening. The city was crowded with many refugees. At last they were safe with friends, who were waiting for them and gave them a hearty welcome.

But they did not stay in Shanghai. After a few days, Dr. Huntley came into the sitting room one morning with a paper in his hand.

"The call has come for Red Cross doctors and nurses to go to Hankow," he said. "The wounded soldiers of both armies are being taken there, and there is no one to care for them. I'm going to volunteer to return as a Red Cross surgeon."

"I'll go with you as a Red Cross nurse," said Jennie Crawford.

"Take me too!" begged Jennie Cody.

"No Americans except doctors and nurses are allowed to enter the city," answered Dr. Huntley.

Jennie Cody looked up at him. "The one thing I have said I never, never could be is a nurse, but I won't be a coward when Jennie Crawford needs help, and wounded soldiers have no one to nurse them. Pin the red cross on my arm, and maybe that will give me courage."

When they bought tickets, the agent said, "You go at your own risk. I can make no promise that you will ever reach Hankow. Many boats are being fired on."

But as the boat with the red cross on its white flag went up the river, the soldiers of both armies lowered their guns.

Such a different Hankow they found! The crowded streets were deserted—even the beggars were gone. The smoke still hung over the ruins of many buildings which had been burned. The fire had not touched an unfinished hospital, and in it they found many wounded soldiers. Most of the fighting was in Hanyang, and the Red Cross launches brought the wounded men of both armies across the river.

Two nurses were already there for day duty, so Jennie Crawford and Jennie Cody slept in the day and went on duty at night, going up and down between the rows of soldiers like angels of mercy. There were few beds, and most of the men had to lie on straw on the floor with no sheets or pillows.

"Which way will it go?" said Jennie Cody one day.

"No one can tell," answered Jennie Crawford. "Just now the revolutionists are ahead. They have captured the arsenal in Hanyang. Three hundred of their soldiers went up to the gate with their clothes torn and looking as if they had been in a battle. They pretended to be the soldiers of the emperor who had been defeated. The gatekeepers let them in, and they took charge of the arsenal without firing a single shot. Now the people are so sure the revolutionists will win that many men have already cut off their queues. The soldiers with swords in their hands demand that men prove they are loyal to the new republic by having their queues cut off."

Virtue Study

Work on 1 Timothy 4:12, the memory verse for this week.

1. What did Miss Crawford and her friends do after they were safe?
2. Why did they choose to serve others instead of staying out of the fighting zone?
3. How did they help the wounded soldiers?
4. What virtues did Miss Crawford have?

Miss Crawford showed love to the people she nursed. What do these verses say about love?
- Luke 6:27–36
- Romans 12:9–13
- Romans 13:8–10
- 1 Corinthians 16:14
- Galatians 5:6b
- Ephesians 4:2

WEEK 12 ~ DAY 4

Upheaval in China, Part 4
By Katharine S. Cronk and Elsie Singmaster, 1921

"If we could only get back to Hanyang again to get some warm clothes!" sighed Jennie Cody. "I'm almost frozen without my winter coat."

"Let's try to go over with Dr. Huntley in the Red Cross launch," proposed Jennie Crawford. "None of the soldiers of either army will fire on that."

When they reached Hanyang, they saw empty rickshaws along the riverbank and many other signs of a hasty retreat. Before they reached their home, a man ran toward them.

"You must be ready to leave at a moment's notice," he cried. "The soldiers of the emperor have taken the city again."

In the dining room the teacups still stood on the table, but they did not stop to put them away. Hastily gathering a few garments, they hurried back to the boat.

Before the boat could pull out, the bullets were falling close beside them. Within half an hour, a terrible battle was fought between the troops of the emperor on the Hankow side of the river and those of the revolutionists on the other side. Nearer and nearer to the hospital came the bullets. One day, the two nurses were awakened by the sound of shells directly over their heads. A bullet struck the wall of the room. Jennie Cody picked it up with a smile that showed she was not afraid, and she put it away for a souvenir. The little Red Cross launches brought in more and yet more wounded soldiers until the nurses could scarcely step between the beds of straw.

After the troops of the emperor had captured Hanyang, they took Hankow and Wuchang. It seemed that the revolution had failed and that the yellow flag with its Manchu dragon would still float above China.

"Look at that man!" said Jennie Crawford one day. "He cut off his queue when he thought the revolutionists had won. Then when the soldiers of the emperor recaptured the city, he was afraid they would cut off his head if they saw him without a queue, and he pinned one to his cap."

"Many men have done that," answered Jennie Cody. "When they think the soldiers of the emperor are going to win, they let their queues hang down their backs. Then if they think victory is going to the revolutionists, they tuck them up under their caps."

"The days may seem dark for the new republic, but even though the arsenal has been captured by the soldiers of the emperor, good news comes from Shanghai and Nanking," said Jennie Crawford. "Everywhere the people are demanding that China shall be free. Shanghai has been taken by the revolutionists without any fighting, and Nanking has already been made the capital of the new government."

Jennie Crawford's prophecy came true. When in 1912 New Year's Day came to China (this time on January 1st by law), Mr. Sun Yat-Sen was inaugurated as the first president of the great Chinghwa (Chinese) Republic, and the dragon flag came down.

Instead, there floated a rainbow flag with stripes of five colors to represent the five peoples of China. There was a red stripe for the Chinese, a blue stripe for the Mongols, a white stripe for the Mohammedans, and a black stripe for the Tibetans. Instead of killing all the Manchu soldiers and the boy emperor, the new republic put a fifth stripe of yellow in its flag for the Manchu people, who were to be a part of the new republic.

When the news reached the two nurses, Miss Crawford said to Miss Cody, "Now I can get back to my own hospital in Hanyang, to all the women and children who are waiting for me." But for many weeks they stayed to nurse the men who could not be moved.

One day they received a command from General Li Yuan Hung, vice president of the new republic, to come to Wuchang, which was thronged with people from many nations: England, France, America, Germany, Russia, Italy, Japan, and Sweden. There, the vice president presented to them bronze medals "in recognition of their bravery and self-sacrifice, in caring for the wounded during the revolution."

"I have almost forgotten the noise of battle and those days in the hospital," said Jennie Crawford as they went back to Hanyang. "But I can never forget that Chinese soldier who looked up at us one night as we tried to ease his pain, and said, 'You are like God to us.'

"'Oh, no,' I answered at once.

"'Well,' said he, as I smoothed his pillow of straw, 'you are the ones who make us know about God.'

"Now I can answer you that I'm still glad I came to China."

Virtue Study

Work on 1 Timothy 4:12, the memory verse for this week.

1. How did Miss Crawford get warmer clothes?
2. Why was the Red Cross boat not attacked?
3. What did Miss Crawford do when the fighting was over?
4. What did the soldier say about Miss Crawford?

What do these verses say about being an example?
- John 13:14–17
- 1 Corinthians 11:1
- 1 Thessalonians 3:7–9
- 1 Timothy 4:11–16
- Titus 2:7a
- 1 Peter 2:21

Box of Visual Reminders

Put a pretty teacup and saucer in your box! These may be purchased from a secondhand store, or you can use one you already have. Tea was an important part of life in China. When you see the cup, remember Jennie's story of courage and service.

WEEK 12 ~ DAY 5

An Indian Princess of the Forest
By James Baldwin, 1896

Pocahontas was born in about 1594. She was the daughter of the powerful Indian chief, Powhatan.

There was once a very brave man whose name was John Smith. He came to this country when there were great woods everywhere, and many Indians and wild beasts. One day when Smith was in the woods, some Indians came upon him and made him their prisoner. They led him to their king, and in a short time they planned to put him to death.

A large stone was brought in, and Smith was made to lie down with his head on it. Then two tall Indians with big clubs in their hands came forward. The king and all his great men stood around to see. The Indians raised their clubs to kill him.

But just then, a little Indian girl rushed in. She was the daughter of the king, and her name was Pocahontas. She ran and threw herself between Smith and the uplifted clubs. She clasped Smith's head with her arms, and she laid her own head upon his.

"Oh, Father!" she cried. "Spare this man's life. I am sure he has done you no harm, and we ought to be his friends."

The men with the clubs could not strike, for they did not want to hurt the child. The king at first did not know what to do. Then he spoke to some of his warriors, and they lifted Smith from the ground. They untied the cords from his wrists and feet and set him free.

The next day, the king sent Smith home, and several Indians went with him to protect him from harm.

For three or four years after this, Pocahontas continued to assist the settlers in their distresses and to shield them from the effects of her father's hostility. Although she was a great favorite with her father, he was so displeased with her for favoring the whites that he sent her away to a chief of a neighboring tribe, Jopazaws, chief of Potowmac, for safekeeping. Or, as some suppose, to avert the anger of her own tribe, who might have been tempted to revenge themselves upon her for her friendship to the English.

Here she remained some time, when Captain Argall, who ascended the Potomac on a trading expedition, tempted the chief by the offer of a large copper kettle to deliver her to him as a prisoner. Argall believed that by having her in his possession as a hostage, he could bring Powhatan to terms of peace. But Powhatan refused to ransom his daughter upon the terms proposed. Instead, he offered five hundred bushels of corn for her, but it was not accepted.

Pocahontas was well treated while a prisoner. During the period of her stay at Jamestown, John Rolfe, an honest and discreet young Englishman, felt that he should strive to make her a Christian. After a time in prayer, he resolved to labor for the conversion of the Indian maiden. The youthful princess received instruction with meekness, and soon, in the little church at Jamestown which rested on rough pine columns fresh from the forest, she stood before the congregation and openly renounced her country's idolatry, professed the faith of Jesus Christ, and was baptized.

The gaining of this one soul, the first convert in Virginia, was followed by a change in name for the Indian princess. She received the Christian name of Rebecca.

Mr. John Rolfe became attached to her and offered her his hand in marriage. The offer was communicated to Powhatan, who gave his consent to the union, and she was married to Rolfe in the presence of her uncle and two brothers. This event relieved the colony from the hostility of Powhatan and preserved peace for many years between them.

In the year 1616, Pocahontas accompanied her husband to England, where she was presented at court and became an object of curiosity and interest to all classes. Her title of princess caused her to receive much attention.

Captain Smith wrote a memorial to the queen in her behalf, setting forth the services which the Indian princess had rendered to him and the colony, which secured her the friendship of the queen.

Pocahontas survived but little more than a year after her arrival in England. She died in 1617, at Gravesend, when about to embark for her native land.

Pocahontas was the first North American Indian who was converted to Christianity by the English settlers. The religion of the gospel seemed pleasant to her nature, and she was like a guardian angel to the white strangers who had come to the land of her people.

Virtue Study

Recite 1 Timothy 4:12, the memory verse for this week.

1. How did Pocahontas help the white men?
2. What happened when she was captured by the English?
3. Who undertook to teach her about God?
4. Pocahontas was the first Indian to become a Christian in Virginia. What does this show us about her character?
5. What virtues did she have?

Pocahontas became a Christian because John Rolfe taught her about Jesus. We as Christians are also called to tell others about Him. Read these verses. How did the leaders teach others about God?

- ♥ Acts 8:30–38
- ♥ Acts 11:20–26
- ♥ Acts 16:13–14

WEEK 13 ~ DAY 1

The Saving of Clotilda
By Elbridge Streeter Brooks, 1911

It was in the year of our Lord 485 that a little girl crouched, trembling and terrified, at the feet of a pitying priest in the palace of the kings of Burgundy. The fair-haired Princess Clotilda had a good reason for terror and tears. Her cruel uncle, Gundebald, waging war against his brother Chilperic, the rightful king of Burgundy, had with a band of savage followers burst into the palace, and after the fierce and relentless fashion of those cruel days, had murdered King Chilperic, the father of little Clotilda; the queen, her mother; and the young princes, her brothers; and was now searching for her and her sister Sedelenda to kill them also.

Poor Sedelenda had hidden away in some other far-off corner, but even as Clotilda hung for protection to the robe of the good priest Ugo of Rheims, the clash of steel drew nearer and nearer. Through the corridor came the rush of feet, the curtain over the doorway was rudely flung aside, and the poor child's fierce pursuers, with her cruel uncle at their head, rushed into the room.

"Here hides the game!" he cried in savage exultation. "Thrust her away, Sir Priest, or thou diest in her stead. Not one of the tyrant's brood shall live. I say it!"

"And who art thou to judge of life or death?" demanded the priest sternly as he still shielded the trembling child.

"I am Gundebald, king of Burgundy by the grace of mine own good sword and the right of succession," was the reply. "Trifle not with me, Sir Priest, but thrust away the child. She is my lawful prize to do with as I will. Ho, Sigebert, drag her forth!"

Quick as a flash the brave priest stepped before the cowering child, and with one hand still resting protecting on the girl's fair hair, he raised the other in stern and fearless protest and boldly faced the murderous throng.

"Back, men of blood!" he cried. "Back! Nor dare to lay a hand on this young maid who hath here sought sanctuary in the church!"

Fierce and savage men always respect bravery in others. There was something so courageous and heroic in the act of that single priest in thus facing a fierce and determined band in defense of a little girl—for girls were but slightingly regarded in those far-off days—that it caught the savage fancy of the cruel king. And this, joined with his respect for the Church's right of sanctuary, and with the lessening of his thirst for blood now that he had satisfied his first desire for revenge, led him to stop.

"So be it then," he said, lowering his threatening sword. "I yield her to thee, Sir Priest. Look to her welfare and thine own. Surely a girl can do no harm."

But King Gundebald and his house lived to learn how far wrong was that unguarded statement. For the very lowering of the murderous sword that thus brought life to the little Princess Clotilda meant the downfall of the kingdom of Burgundy and the rise of the great and victorious nation of France. The memories of even a little maid of ten are not easily blotted out.

Her sister, Sedelenda, had found refuge and safety in the convent of Ainay. Clotilda wished to join her, but her uncle, the new king, said, "No, the maidens must be separated forever." He expressed a willingness to have the Princess Clotilda brought up in his palace, which had been her father's, and requested the priest Ugo of Rheims to remain awhile and look after the girl's education.

In those days a king's request was a command, and the good Ugo, though stern and brave in the face of real danger, was wise enough to know that it was best for him to yield to the king's wishes. So he continued in the palace of the king, looking after the welfare of his little charge, until suddenly the girl took matters into her own hands and decided his future and her own.

The kingdom of Burgundy, in the days of the Princess Clotilda, was a large tract of country now embraced by southern France and western Switzerland. It had been given by the Romans to the Goths, who had invaded it in the year 413. It was a land of forest and vineyards, of fair valleys and sheltered hillsides, and of busy cities that the fostering hand of Rome had beautified; while through its broad domain the Rhone, pure and sparkling, swept with a rapid current from Swiss lake and glacier southward to the broad and beautiful Mediterranean. Lyons was its capital, and on the hill of Fourviere, overlooking the city below it, rose the marble palace of the Burgundian kings.

But the palace no longer felt like home to the little Princess Clotilda. She thought of her father and mother, and of her brothers, the little princes with whom she had played in this very palace, as it now seemed to her, so many years ago. The more she feared her cruel uncle, the more she desired to go far, far away from his presence. So after thinking the whole matter over, she told her good friend Ugo of her father's youngest brother Godegesil, who ruled the dependent principality of Geneva, far up the valley of the Rhone.

"Yes, child, I know the place," said Ugo. "A fair city indeed, on the blue and beautiful Lake Lemanus, walled in by mountains and rich in corn and vineyards."

"Then let us fly there," said the girl. "My uncle Godegesil I know will help us, and I shall be freed from my fears of King Gundebald."

Virtue Study

Memory Verse: 1 Timothy 6:12. Write this verse on a 3 x 5 card and memorize it during the week.

1. Why did Clotilda's uncle want to kill her?
2. How was she rescued?
3. Why did she want to leave the palace?

The kind priest who saved her gives us a picture of what Jesus has done for us. We deserved death, but Jesus stood in the gap and saved us. What do these verses say about God's saving nature?
- ♥ 1 Corinthians 15:1–10a
- ♥ 1 Timothy 2:3–6
- ♥ 2 Timothy 1:8–10
- ♥ Titus 3:4–8

WEEK 13 ~ DAY 2

The Service of Clotilda
By Elbridge Streeter Brooks, 1911

Though going to her uncle seemed at first to the good priest only a child's desire, he learned to think better of it when he saw how unhappy the poor girl was in the hated palace, and how slight were her chances for improvement. And so, one fair spring morning in the year 486, the two slipped quietly out of the palace, and by slow and cautious stages, with help from friendly priests and nuns and frequent rides in the heavy ox wagons that were the only means of transport other than horseback, they finally reached the old city of Geneva.

On the journey, the good Ugo made the road seem less weary, and the lumbering ox wagons less jolty and painful, by telling his bright young charge of all the wonders and relics he had seen in his journeying in the East. She especially loved to hear him tell of the boy-king of the Franks, Clovis, who lived in the priest's own boyhood home of Tournay, in Belgium, and who, though so brave and daring, was still a pagan when all the world was fast becoming Christian. And as Clotilda listened, she wished that she could turn this brave young chief away from his heathen deities, Thor and

Odin, to the worship of the Christians' God. But even as they reached the fair city of Geneva, the wonderful news met them how this boy-king, Clovis, had sent a challenge of combat to the prefect Syagrius, the last of the Roman governors, and how he had defeated him in a battle at Soissons and broken forever the power of Rome in Gaul.

War, which is never anything but terrible, was doubly so in those savage days, and the plunder of the captured cities was the chief return for which the barbarian soldiers followed their leaders. But when the Princess Clotilda heard how, even in the midst of his burning and plundering, the young Frankish chief spared some of the fairest Christian churches, he became still more her hero; and again the desire to convert him from paganism took shape in her mind.

The good priest Ugo of Rheims saw that his own homeland was in trouble, and he felt that his duty lay there. Godegesil was uneasy from the nearness of this youthful conqueror and the possible displeasure of his brother and overlord, King Gundebald, and so he declined longer to shelter his niece in his palace at Geneva.

"And why may I not go with you?" the girl asked of Ugo, but the old priest knew that a conquered and plundered land was no place to take a young maid for safety, and the princess, therefore, found refuge among the sisters of the church of St. Peter in Geneva. And here she passed her girlhood, as the record says, "in works of piety and charity."

So four more years went by. In the north, the young chieftain, reaching manhood, had been raised up on the shields of his fair-haired and long-limbed followers, and with many a shout had been proclaimed "King of the Franks." In the south, the young Princess Clotilda, now nearly sixteen, had washed the feet of pilgrims, ministered to the poor, and proved herself a zealous church worker in that low-roofed convent near the old church of St. Peter.

One bright summer day, as the young princess passed into the guest room for poor pilgrims attached to the convent, she saw there a stranger dressed in rags. He had the wallet and staff of a begging pilgrim, and coming toward her, he asked for "charity in the name of the blessed St. Peter, whose church thou servest."

The young girl brought the pilgrim food, and then, according to the custom of the day, kneeling on the earthen floor, she began to bathe his feet. But as she did so, the pilgrim, bending forward, said in a low voice, "Lady, I have great matters to announce to thee, if thou wish me to reveal them."

Pilgrims in those days were frequently made the bearers of special messages between distant friends, but this poor young orphan princess could think of no one from whom a message to her might come. Nevertheless, she simply said, "Say on."

In the same low tone the beggar continued, "Clovis, King of the Franks, sends thee greeting."

The girl looked up now, thoroughly surprised. This beggar must be a madman, she thought. But the eyes of the pilgrim looked at her reassuringly, and he said, "In token whereof, he sendeth thee this ring by me, his confidant and trusted bodyguard, Aurelian of Soissons."

The Princess Clotilda took, as if in a dream, the ring of transparent jacinth set in solid gold, and asked quietly, "What would the king of the Franks want with me?"

"The king, my master, hath heard from the holy Bishop Remi and the good priest Ugo of thy beauty and discreetness," replied Aurelian, "and likewise of the sad condition of one who is the daughter of a royal line. He bade me use all my wit to come nigh to thee, and to say that, if it be the will of the gods, he would fain raise thee to his rank by marriage."

Those were days of swift and sudden surprises, when kings made up their minds in royal haste, and princesses were not expected to be surprised at whatever they might hear. All the dreams of her younger days came into the girl's mind, and as the record states, "she accepted the ring with great joy."

Virtue Study

Work on 1 Timothy 6:12, the memory verse for this week.

1. What did Clotilda do while she was young?
2. How did she spend her time?
3. What virtues did she have?

Clotilda was following the example of Jesus by washing the feet of pilgrims who visited the church. Read John 13:1–5 and 13:12–17. Why did Jesus wash the disciples' feet?

If Clotilda had been a conceited princess who thought such lowly work beneath her, what would she have missed?

WEEK 13 ~ DAY 3

The Husband of Clotilda
By Elbridge Streeter Brooks, 1911

"Return promptly to thy lord," she said to the messenger, "and bid him, if he would fain unite me to him in marriage, to send messengers without delay to demand me of my uncle, King Gundebald, and let those same messengers take me away in haste, as soon as they shall have obtained permission."

This wise young princess knew that her uncle's word was not to be long depended upon, and she feared, too, that certain advisers at her uncle's court might counsel him to do her harm before the messengers of King Clovis could conduct her beyond the borders of Burgundy.

Aurelian, still in his pilgrim's disguise (for he feared discovery in a hostile country), hastened back to King Clovis, who, the record says, was "pleased with his success and with Clotilda's notion, and at once sent a delegation to Gundebald to demand his niece in marriage."

As Clotilda foresaw, her uncle stood in too much dread of this fierce young conqueror of the north to say him nay. "Now deliver the princess into our hand, King Gundebald," said the messenger,

Aurelian, "that we may take her to King Clovis, who waiteth for us even now at Chalons to conclude these nuptials."

So, almost before he knew what he was doing, King Gundebald had bidden his niece farewell. And the princess, with her escort of Frankish spears, was rumbling away in a clumsy covered ox wagon toward the frontier of Burgundy.

But the slow-moving ox wagon by no means suited the impatience of this clever young princess. She knew her uncle, the king of Burgundy, too well. When once he was roused to action, he was fierce and furious.

"Good Aurelian," she said at length to the king's ambassador, who rode by her side, "if thou wouldst take me into the presence of thy lord, the king of the Franks, let me descend from this carriage, mount me on horseback, and let us speed hence as fast as we may, for never in this carriage shall I reach the presence of my lord the king."

And none too soon was her advice acted upon, for the counselors of King Gundebald noticed Clotilda's anxiety to be gone and concluded that, after all, they had made a mistake in betrothing her to King Clovis.

Forthwith the king sent off an armed band with orders to bring back both the princess and the treasure he had sent with her as her marriage gift. But already the princess and her escort were safely across the Seine, where she met the king of the Franks.

From the midst of his fur-clad and green-robed guards and nobles, young Clovis—in a dress of crimson and gold, and milk-white silk, and with his yellow hair coiled in a great knot on his uncovered head—advanced to meet his bride.

"My Lord King," said Clotilda, "the soldiers of the king of Burgundy follow hard upon us to bear me off. Command, I pray thee, that thy men scatter and attack them."

Probably in no other way could this wise young girl of seventeen have so thoroughly pleased the fierce and warlike young king. He gladly ordered her wishes to be carried out. So her troubles were ended, and this king and princess, in spite of the wicked uncle Gundebald, were married at Soissons in the year 493.

Her longing to convert Clovis began immediately after their marriage. Through patience and love she tried to share the love of the Savior with her husband, but all her efforts fell on deaf ears. Her husband had no interest in such matters.

The good woman, in no way discouraged, did the most powerful thing a girl or woman can do—she began praying for her husband. One day, Clovis and his followers went out to fight the Alemanni, a fierce Germanic tribe. In the battle things started to go against King Clovis, and it appeared that the day might be lost.

Hopelessly, King Clovis looked around, but there was no one to help him. His men were being pushed back. Then, in a moment of despair, he called upon the God of his wife. "Most Mighty God whom my Queen Clotilda worships and adores with all her heart and soul, I pledge my perpetual service to your faith. Please give me now the victory over my enemies." When he had finished his prayer, he looked up and saw his army, who had moments before been retreating, now fighting with power. The king of the enemy was killed, and his followers lost heart.

The Lord brought about a great victory for King Clovis that day. At a celebration banquet, King Clovis made a humble declaration: "Lords of the Franks, it seems to me highly profitable that ye should know, first of all, that the gods we formerly worshiped are false and powerless. There is only one God and one power over man. Know of a surety that this same God, the one whom our queen embraces, is my God now. He it was who delivered us when all was lost on the battlefield. He gave us victory, and now the kingdom of the Franks is united. Lift therefore your hearts in just hope, and ask the Sovereign Defender that He give you all that which you desire, that He save your souls and give us victory over our enemies." King Clovis and three thousand of the Franks were baptized. The simple prayers of a virtuous woman changed the country.

Virtue Study

Work on 1 Timothy 6:12, the memory verse for this week.

1. How did Clotilda escape from the grip of her uncle?
2. How did she influence her husband and his people?
3. What virtues did she have?

The Bible clearly states that a believer should never marry an unbeliever. The culture that Clotilda lived in was very different from today. If she had waited for her uncle to pick out her husband, it is probable that she would have ended up with an unbeliever. She bravely sought refuge with a husband of her own choosing whom she could respect.

What do these verses say about marriage?
- ♥ 1 Corinthians 7:39
- ♥ 2 Corinthians 6:14

We have already read Proverbs 31:10–31, but let's read it again. How did Clotilda model the virtues of the woman in Proverbs?

WEEK 13 ~ DAY 4

The Hiding Place
By Mr. Blaisdell and Mr. Ball, 1921

There is a little river in Kentucky called Dreaming Creek, and many years ago a fort was built near the river. In a log cabin about two miles from the fort lived Amos Hopkins and his family.

The Hopkins family consisted of father, mother, and three children. The oldest child, Joseph, was a sturdy boy of fourteen. He could use a rifle nearly as well as his father. Polly, a lively girl of twelve, was nicknamed "Long-Legged Polly" because she could run so fast. Peter, the youngest child, was about six years old.

One day, Polly Hopkins crept under a vine on the trunk of the old tree and suddenly disappeared.

"Oh, Polly, where are you?" cried Joe.

"Come quick, Joe, and see what I have found."

So Joe crawled after his sister. He found himself inside the tree.

"Oh, my," cried Polly, "what a splendid place to play on rainy days or to hide from the Indians!" They made a clean floor of oak leaves and pine needles, and used dry moss for seats.

It was a lovely day in June, a few years after the close of the Revolution. Mr. Hopkins was away, and Mrs. Hopkins was busy about the house. The children were playing in the open space in front of the cabin because it was Polly's birthday.

"Now, Joe," said Mrs. Hopkins, "you children may have your birthday party down by the river in your beech-tree house. Look sharp after little Peter and see that he doesn't get hurt."

"All right, Mother. I won't let him get lost or fall into the river."

The big beech tree down by the river was well-known to the children. They often spent the afternoon there, playing in its shade.

The three children hurried down the trail to the river. In the shade of the tree they ate their luncheon and played their games. After a time they crept into the hollow in the tree and told stories until sunset. Little Peter grew tired and was put to sleep on a pile of dry moss.

"Why, Polly," said Joe, "I forgot to bring my rifle. I will run back to the cabin and get it. There may be Indians prowling about after dark. Don't stir till I come back."

Polly climbed up on a shelf that Joe had built and looked out of a hole in the tree. She watched Joe until he went through the open gate of the stockade. In a few minutes he and his mother ran out of the cabin and shut the big gate. Polly sat down beside Peter and waited. Still Joe did not return.

"What can be the matter with him?" asked Polly. "Why did they shut the gate in such a hurry? Can there be Indians about? Dear me, I wish he would come. I'll take one more look."

Before long she saw the bushes across the way gently moving. In another moment, a tall Indian in war paint and feathers rose silently and came walking toward the old beech tree. After looking round the tree and peeping into the branches, he quietly glided into the underbrush. Polly knew her danger and stood still. She hardly dared to draw a deep breath. Looking again, she saw half a dozen Indians creeping along the trail toward the cabin. *Crack,* sounded

Joe's rifle, and a warrior fell dead. The other Indians ran out with dry moss and threw lighted bundles onto the roof of the cabin. Polly's heart began to beat faster.

"There is just one thing to do. I must run to the fort and get Captain Zane and his men."

With one little sob, she looked at her brother quietly sleeping on the moss. Then she crept through the opening and into the underbrush until she found the trail to the fort. She was frightened, but she darted away in the direction of the fort.

It was dark now, and the trail was narrow. At any moment a lurking warrior might jump out of the underbrush. On and on she ran, as never before. It seemed hours, but it was only minutes. Once, she was out of breath and fell panting to the ground. It was only for a moment. She picked herself up and started on again.

Just as she seemed ready to fall in a faint, she reached the fort, high up on the bank of the river. She was seen by the riflemen on guard when she ran toward the big oak gate.

"Indians! The Hopkins cabin! Quick! Quick!" she cried.

The riflemen crowded round her to hear her story. "There is no time to spare," said Captain Zane to his men. "Look well to your horses and rifles. We are in for a lively scrap with the Indians before sunrise."

In a few minutes, twenty sturdy Indian fighters were galloping down the trail as fast as their hardy little horses could carry them. Captain Zane had taken Polly up behind him.

Mr. Hopkins had come back home while the children were playing in the old beech tree. Now he and Joe were making it lively for the enemy, firing their rifles from the loopholes in the stockade.

With shouts, the riflemen fell on the warriors. The Indians, leaving their dead and wounded behind them, fled into the woods. A few buckets of water put out the fire on the roof.

"Where is Peter?" asked Mrs. Hopkins.

"Why, Mother, I had almost forgotten him," answered Polly. "Come, Joe, let us run down to the old beech tree." They found the boy still asleep on the pile of moss.

"I had a bad dream," said Peter. "I thought the Indians were chasing me and had grabbed me just as Joe and Polly found me."

Virtue Study

Work on 1 Timothy 6:12, the memory verse for this week.

1. How did the Hopkins children discover the hiding place?
2. Polly had a skill. What was it?
3. What did Polly do when her family was in danger?

God gives each of us talents that He wants us to use. What do these verses say about doing everything wholeheartedly?
- ♥ Ecclesiastes 9:10a
- ♥ Colossians 3:23–24

Just as the Hopkins children found a hiding place, the Bible talks about God being our hiding place. What promises are found in these verses?
- ♥ Psalm 17:8
- ♥ Psalm 32:7

Does Polly remind you of anyone in the Bible? Read Exodus 2:1–10. How did Moses's sister help her family?

WEEK 13 ~ DAY 5

Grace Darling's Heroic Deed
By James Baldwin, 1896

It was a dark September morning. There was a storm at sea. A ship had been driven on a low rock off the shores of the Farne Islands. It had been broken in two by the waves, and half of it had been washed away. The other half lay yet on the rock, and those of the crew who were still alive were clinging to it. But the waves were dashing over it, and in a little while it too would be carried to the bottom.

Could anyone save the poor, half-drowned men who were there?

On one of the islands was a lighthouse, and there, all through that stormy night, Grace Darling had listened to the storm. Grace was the daughter of the lighthouse keeper, and she had lived by the sea as long as she could remember.

In the darkness of the night, above the noise of the winds and waves, she heard screams and wild cries. When daylight came, she could see the wreck, a mile away, with the angry waters all around it. She could see the men clinging to the masts.

"We must try to save them!" she cried. "Let us go out in the boat at once!"

"It is of no use, Grace," said her father. "We cannot reach them."

He was an old man, and he knew the force of the mighty waves.

"We cannot stay here and see them die," said Grace. "We must at least try to save them."

Her father could not say no. In a few minutes they were ready. They set off in the heavy lighthouse boat. Grace pulled one oar, and her father the other, and they made straight toward the wreck. But it was hard rowing against such a sea, and it seemed as though they would never reach the place.

At last they were close to the rock, and now they were in greater danger than before. The fierce waves broke against the boat, and it would have been dashed to pieces had it not been for the strength and skill of the brave girl.

After many attempts, Grace's father climbed upon the wreck, while Grace herself held the boat. Then, one by one, the worn-out crew were helped on board. It was all that the girl could do to keep the boat from being drifted away or broken upon the sharp edges of the rock.

Then her father clambered back into his place. Strong hands grasped the oars, and by and by all were safe in the lighthouse.

There Grace proved to be no less tender as a nurse than she had been brave as a sailor. She cared most kindly for the shipwrecked men until the storm had died away and they were strong enough to go to their own homes.

All this happened a long time ago, but the name of Grace Darling will never be forgotten. She lies buried now in a little churchyard by the sea, not far from her old home. Every year many people go there to see her grave, and there a monument has been placed in honor of the brave girl. It is not a large monument, but it is one that speaks of the noble deed which made Grace Darling famous. It is a figure carved in stone of a woman lying at rest, with a boat's oar held fast in her right hand.

Virtue Study

Recite 1 Timothy 6:12, the memory verse for this week.

1. Where did Grace live?
2. What did she do when she saw the shipwreck?
3. How did she show her bravery?
4. What virtues did she have?

God created the sea. The awesome power of the ocean is nothing compared to His power. Look up these verses and discuss what they mean.

- ♥ Job 11:7–9
- ♥ Psalm 93:3–4
- ♥ Psalm 95:4–5
- ♥ John 17:11
- ♥ Romans 1:19–20
- ♥ 2 Corinthians 13:3–4
- ♥ Ephesians 3:16–21
- ♥ Philippians 3:10–11

Box of Visual Reminders

Grace helped her father keep the lighthouse running. The Bible tells us that we are supposed to be a light to those around us. Put a candle in your box to remind you to shine for Him.

LIST OF VIRTUES

Appreciative	Faithful	Obedient
Attentive	Fearless	Optimistic
Brave	Flexible	Patient
Calm	Forgiving	Peaceful
Cheerful	Generous	Persevering
Committed	Gentle	Persistent
Compassionate	Giving	Persuasive
Concerned	Good	Prepared
Congenial	Gracious	Prudent
Considerate	Honest	Ready
Consistent	Humble	Resolute
Content	Initiative	Resourceful
Cooperative	Inspiring	Respectful
Courageous	Integrity	Responsible
Creative	Joyful	Self-controlled
Decisive	Kind	Sincere
Dependable	Longsuffering	Submissive
Diligent	Loving	Tactful
Discerning	Loyal	Thorough
Discreet	Meek	Thrifty
Efficient	Merciful	Truthful
Encouraging	Observant	Willing

Other Books by Amy Puetz

Costumes with Character: Make Your Own Costumes from Eleven Time Periods with One Dress! It is Easy to Make Historical Costumes with Only One Dress! Are you ready to make history come alive? This easy sewing book has patterns and step-by-step instructions for making accessories for eleven different time periods. Brave the wilderness in an authentic looking pioneer bonnet, attend a tea party in a Victorian collar, and help America win the Revolution dressed in a vest. These are just a few of the time periods covered in this innovative book.

Uncover Exciting History: Revealing America's Christian Heritage in Short, Easy-to-Read Nuggets

What is history anyway? It is the story of real people who did real things. For history to be fun for everyone it must go beyond hard facts and meaningless dates to the real people who made the significant events happen. People like George Washington, who bravely crossed the partly frozen Delaware River to attack the British at Trenton. Stories like that of the bold Americans who bravely fought against the Barbary pirates during the little-known Barbary War show how interesting history is.

www.AmyPuetz.com

www.ingramcontent.com/pod-product-compliance
Lightning Source LLC
Chambersburg PA
CBHW031238290426
44109CB00012B/341